ELEMENTARY

A NEW TRIP AROUND THE WORLD

Activities Across the Curriculum for Puerto Rico, Guatemala, Cuba, Peru, Chile, Spain, the United Kingdom, Norway, Iraq, Afghanistan, Ghana, and Morocco

D1517219

by
Leland Graham, PhD, and Isabelle McCoy, MEd

Carson-Dellosa Publishing Company, Inc.

Greensboro, North Carolina

Acknowledgements

The authors would like to acknowledge the assistance of the following people:
Jorge Arévalo, Luis Fernandez, Diane LaPointe, Cesar Macedo, and Douglas Rodriguez.

Editor: Carrie Fox

Inside Illustrations: Joe Eckstein, Nancy White Cassidy, Erik Huffine, Nick Greenwood, and Ray Lambert

Cover and Layout Design: Nick Greenwood

© 2008, Carson-Dellosa Publishing Company, Inc., Greensboro, North Carolina 27425. The purchase of this material entitles the buyer to reproduce worksheets and activities for classroom use only—not for commercial resale. Reproduction of these materials for an entire school or district is prohibited. No part of this book may be reproduced (except as noted above), stored in a retrieval system, or transmitted in any form or by any means (mechanically, electronically, recording, etc.) without the prior written consent of Carson-Dellosa Publishing Co., Inc.

Printed in the USA • All rights reserved.

ISBN 978-1-60418-034-3

Table of Contents

Introduction

A New Trip Around the World gives students the opportunity to explore life in Puerto Rico, Guatemala, Cuba, Peru, Chile, Spain, the United Kingdom, Norway, Iraq, Afghanistan, Ghana, and Morocco. The section for each country contains basic information (area, population, flag descriptions, etc.), fascinating facts (sports, education, wildlife, etc.), language activities, recipes, classroom activities, a worksheet, a flag, a map, and a resource list. Below are lists of extension ideas for each type of activity:

Basic Information

- Use the facts to make comparisons. For example, how many Peruvian Nuevo sols equal one American dollar?
- Discuss the countries' histories. Have the native cultures had similar experiences?
- Ask each student to invite an adult family member to share experiences about the history of his or her family's homeland.
- Graph the types of land formations in each country. How many countries have deserts, tropical zones, etc.?
- Make a list of all of the natural resources that are cultivated in each country. Students can also discuss what life would be like for their country and other countries if they did not have certain resources.
- Compare the different types of governments in the countries. Nations like Iraq and Afghanistan have undergone great political and social change. Have students pretend that they are developing a new country. Tell them to choose what type of government they would like to establish in their new land.

Fascinating Facts

- Write each fascinating fact on an index card. Laminate the cards. Then, use the cards to play a trivia game.
- Create traditional art for each country. Have students design a mask, make a puppet, make a drum, etc.
- Use the information as topics for oral or written reports. Have advanced students compare the same aspect of two or more countries (sports in Cuba and Iraq, etc.).
- Find pictures of homes or buildings mentioned in this section or in the basic information section. Assign a group of students to each country. Have students build replicas with craft sticks, papier-mâché, grass, straw, clay, etc. Use the buildings to make a global neighborhood.

Language Activities

- Have students create coded messages using words from each country's language. Have them select partners and trade messages.
- Practice using the languages each day. Challenge students to use the words in conversation.
- Create file folder games with different word categories. Have students match all of the number words, ways to say hello, etc. (File folders can also be used to match flags, maps of countries, types of money, etc.).

Recipes*

- Copy the recipes in each section and send one home with each student. Have each student make the recipe with a family member and bring it to school for a multicultural snack. Host an international snack party for another class.
- Have a multicultural bake sale. Ask students and their families to bake their favorite international dishes. Sell the goods and donate the money raised to an international charity organization.

* *Caution:* Before completing any food activity, ask families' permission and inquire about students' food allergies and religious or other food preferences.

© Carson-Dellosa • CD-104263

Classroom Activities

- Have each student make a family tree reaching as far back as possible. Post the trees around the classroom. Do any of the students have ancestors from one or more of the countries studied?
- Using an Internet search engine, locate an elementary school in each country. Contact at least one of the schools and see if the teachers and administrators are willing to start a pen pal program. Or, use a reputable, secure pen pal service on the Internet. Contact the country's embassy for more information.
- Brainstorm story starters for the class. For example, *My favorite country is _____ because . . .*, or *I visited _____ , and I saw . . . .*
- Host a multicultural festival with food, music, dancing, and celebrations from all of the countries. Invite the whole school and make it a yearly event!
- As a class, research one of the countries in depth. When you have gathered all of the research, have students help you put all of the information into a book. Donate the book to the school library. Encourage other classrooms to do the same with other countries.

Worksheets

- Use the worksheets to make file folder games.
- Use the patterns to make finger puppets, necklaces, shape books, Afghan rugs, etc.

Flags

- Use the book's cover and the flag descriptions to compare similarities in the countries' flags. How many of the flags have religious or mythical elements? How many have changed recently?
- After studying the flags, have students brainstorm ideas for a class flag. Have groups design samples for a flag and have them explain the reasons behind their choices. Have the class vote on the design they want to represent the class.
- Have a parade of nations. Have students dress in traditional costumes made from fabric scraps, beads, etc. Have each student make a flag for the country she is dressed to represent.
- Have each student design a flag to represent himself.
- Enlarge, reproduce, color, and display the flags around the room. Check out a copy of a national anthems recording from a local library. Have students choose a flag to study each morning and, if available, play that country's anthem.
- Have a mock United Nations meeting with all of the flags and countries present. Try solving global problems that are currently in the news. (Make sure that the global topics discussed are appropriate for students' ages, comprehension levels, etc.)
- Make floor puzzles from the full-page flag reproducibles. Enlarge, color, cut out, and display each flag on poster board. Then, cut each flag into puzzle pieces and let the fun begin!

Maps

- Enlarge the maps to create bulletin boards or to use as pages for a shape book. On the maps, list cities, neighboring countries, natural resources, topographical regions, ethnic backgrounds, etc.
- Enlarge the maps and trace them onto cardboard. Use plaster of paris, clay, or papier-mâché to create a topographical map of each country. Students can add figures to represent animals, as well as natural resources and industries.

Additional Resources Lists

- While studying each country, have a student help you read one of the books to the class each day.
- Have students pretend that they are the main characters in the books. How would they react to the customs in the home country? How do they like being in the characters' shoes?
- Use the books to compare national holidays. Compare the ways other countries celebrate religious holidays, Independence Day, etc., to the ways Americans celebrate similar holidays.
- Read folktales from each country. Discuss their similarities and differences. Have each student create her own folktale pertaining to a certain country.

First Stop: Puerto Rico

Area: 3,425 sq. miles (8,870 sq. km)
Capital City: San Juan
Population: 3,944,259
Main Languages: Spanish and English
Main Religion: Roman Catholicism
Currency: U.S. dollar
Government: Commonwealth of the U.S.
Flag:

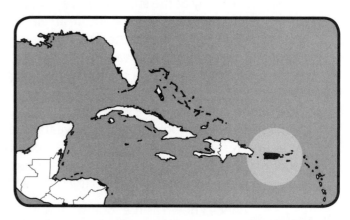

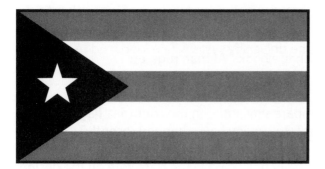

The Puerto Rican flag was adopted in 1952. The flag has five horizontal bands that alternate between red and white, starting with red. In the center of a blue triangle on the hoist side (the side of the flag that is attached to a flagpole or staff) is a large white star. The red stripes symbolize blood, and the white stripes symbolize individual liberty and rights. The blue triangle represents the three branches of government, and the white star represents Puerto Rico.

For Your Information

The Commonwealth of Puerto Rico is located in the northeastern Caribbean. It is east of the Dominican Republic and west of the Virgin Islands, approximately 1,000 miles (1,609 kilometers) off the southern coast of Florida. The archipelago of Puerto Rico includes the main island of Puerto Rico, the smallest of the Greater Antilles, and a number of smaller islands and keys, the largest of which are Mona, Vieques, and Culebra. The capital, San Juan, is located on the main island's north coast. The people of Puerto Rico sometimes refer to their island as "Boriken," a name for the island used by the indigenous Taino people.

The highest point in Puerto Rico is Cerro de Puenta (4,390 feet or 1,339 meters) located in the main mountainous range called *La Cordillera Central* (The Central Range). Another important mountain peak is El Yunque located in the Sierra de Luquillo in the Caribbean National Forest. The Caribbean National Forest, also known as *El Yunque*, is a tropical rain forest and home to more than 240 plants and 50 species of birds.

Puerto Rico has 17 man-made lakes and more than 50 rivers. Most of these rivers begin in the Cordillera Central. The rivers in the north of the island are larger than those in the south. The rivers are smaller in the south due to drier and warmer temperatures.

Tourism is an important part of the Puerto Rican economy. Each year, between one and two million visitors stay at Puerto Rico's hotels and inns, and large numbers of cruise ship passengers also visit the island. Even though Puerto Rico has beautiful beaches and a tropical climate, the country has limited natural resources. Large deposits of copper and some nickel exist in some of Puerto Rico's mountains, but these minerals have not been mined, partly because of environmental concerns.

© Carson-Dellosa • CD-104263

Fascinating Facts

The Caribbean National Forest contains 28,000 acres (113.3 square kilometers) of rain forest and receives more than 100 billion gallons of rainfall each year. Living in the forest is the tiny coquí frog, which receives its name from its cricket-like chirp. This small creature is considered the national mascot.

Puerto Rico has a unique mixture of four cultures: African, Taino (American Indians), Spanish, and North American. From Africans, Puerto Ricans obtained a type of music and dance known as the "bomba and plena." From Taino, Puerto Ricans kept many names for their cities, foods, and other objects. Puerto Ricans received the Spanish language and the Catholic religion from the Spanish people. The university system, fast food, and the English language were brought to the island from North America.

Puerto Rico enjoys an average temperature of 82.4°F (28°C) throughout the year. The seasons do not vary as drastically as in the United States. Temperatures in the south are usually a few degrees warmer than in the north. In the interior mountains, temperatures are always cooler than the rest of the island. Hurricane season lasts from June through November.

Cooking in Puerto Rico is similar to both Spanish and Mexican cuisine; however, it has a unique blend of Spanish, African, Taino, and American influences. Puerto Ricans call their cuisine *Cocina Criolla*, which literally means "Créole kitchen." They use ingredients and seasonings, such as coriander, papaya, cacao, nispero, apio, plantains, and yampee.

Plantains are an important crop in many parts of Puerto Rico. However, there is such a high demand for them that the country also imports plantains from the Dominican Republic and Costa Rica. Plantains look similar to bananas but are larger and thicker.

Banana trees can be found in many backyards in Puerto Rico. Bananas must be cut while they are green and unripe. If not, they will develop a bad taste. Bananas, like plantains, may be prepared either green or ripened.

A favorite fruit on the island is the guava, or *guayaba*. The fruit is round or pear-shaped and contains many small, hard seeds. This large, yellow fruit is eaten when the fruit is ripe. Guava jams, jellies, and preserves are made and eaten on toast for breakfast. Fresh guavas are rich in vitamins A, B, and C. They are eaten raw or sliced and served with sugar and cream as a dessert.

A frozen island treat enjoyed by children is known as *limbers*. This treat is made by freezing any kind of juice in an ice cube tray. In Puerto Rico, the favorite limbers flavors are coconut and guava.

Latin jazz and salsa are enjoyed throughout Puerto Rico. Merengue, rock, rap, *bomba*, and *plena* are also popular on the island. Many musical groups preserve *jíbaro* (folk) music by playing traditional instruments, such as the *cuatro*, *marímbula*, *güiro*, drums, and maracas.

Spanish Language Activities

Colors		Numbers		Days of the Week	
rojo	red	*uno*	one	*lunes*	Monday
azul	blue	*dos*	two	*martes*	Tuesday
amarillo	yellow	*tres*	three	*miércoles*	Wednesday
verde	green	*cuatro*	four	*jueves*	Thursday
anaranjado	orange	*cinco*	five	*viernes*	Friday
rosa	pink	*seis*	six	*sábado*	Saturday
moreno	brown	*siete*	seven	*domingo*	Sunday
blanco	white	*ocho*	eight		
negro	black	*nueve*	nine		
		diez	ten		

The National Anthem of Puerto Rico
"La Borinqueña"

Lyrics by Manuel Fernández Juncos (1846–1928)

The title of this song refers to the name the native Taino people gave to the country, *Boriken* or *Borinquen*.

La tierra de Borinquén	The land of Borinquén
donde he nacido yo,	where I was born,
es un jardín florido	is a flower garden
de mágico fulgor.	of magical brilliance.
Un cielo siempre nítido	An ever-clear sky
le sirve de dosel	serves as a canopy
y dan arrullos plácidos	and placid lullabies are sung
las olas a sus pies.	by the waves at its feet.
Cuando a sus playas llegó Colón;	When Columbus arrived at its beaches,
Exclamó lleno de admiración:	full of admiration he exclaimed:
"Oh!, oh!, oh!	"Oh!, Oh!, Oh!,
esta es la linda tierra que busco yo."	This is the beautiful land that I seek."
Es Borinquén la hija,	Borinquén is the daughter,
la hija del mar y el sol,	the daughter of the sea and the sun,
del mar y el sol,	of the sea and the sun,
del mar y el sol,	of the sea and the sun,
del mar y el sol,	of the sea and the sun,
del mar y el sol.	of the sea and the sun.

© Carson-Dellosa • CD-104263

Recipes

Besitos de Coco (Coconut Kisses)

Ingredients:
2 cups (473 mL) water
4 cups (0.95 L) grated coconut or
    unsweetened coconut flakes
3 cups (710 mL) brown sugar
½ tsp. (2.5 mL) vanilla extract

Directions:
Bring the water and coconut to a boil in a saucepan. Stir thoroughly while adding the brown sugar. Cook on medium-high temperature for approximately 45 minutes. Stir occasionally. As the mixture becomes sticky and harder to stir, add the vanilla flavoring and stir well. Continue cooking for approximately 3–4 minutes until the mixture becomes very sticky. Grease a cookie sheet and drop the mixture by tablespoons onto the greased sheet. Allow to cool completely. Yield: approximately 30 pieces

Platanutres (Plantain Chips)

Ingredients:
4 green plantains
1 tsp. (5 mL) garlic salt
2 cups (473 mL) cooking oil

Directions:
Peel the plantains by removing the ends and cutting lengthwise on the skin. Pry off the skin by sliding the tip of a dull knife into the slit, then push the peel away from the plantain. Wash the plantains after peeling.

Using a metal grater, slice the plantains into thin slices, approximately ¼" (0.64 cm) each. Wash your hands with water, soap, and table salt. (The salt helps remove the *mancha de plátano,* or the "stain of the plantain," as it is called by Puerto Ricans.)

Heat oil until hot. Add the plantain slices and cook over medium heat until golden brown. Remove the plantain chips from the oil and place on paper towels to soak up the excess oil. Add garlic salt to taste. Yield: 4–6 servings

© Carson-Dellosa • CD-104263

Classroom Activities

The most recognizable species and a symbol of Puerto Rican pride is the coquí, a small frog named for the sound it makes. In the Caribbean National Forest, between 13 and 16 species of coquí can be found.

Coquí Frog Puppet

Materials: (per student)
1 coquí frog puppet and tongue pattern (page 11)
2 sheets of green felt
small scraps of red and brown felt
2 wiggle eyes
white school glue
scissors
pencil or fine marker for tracing

Directions:
Make one copy of the frog and tongue pattern for each student. Have each student cut out the frog pattern. Then, have her place the pattern on top of one sheet of the green felt and trace. Have each student repeat with the second piece of green felt. Next, ask each student to cut out each frog from the felt and glue the edges together, leaving an opening for her to insert her hand at the bottom. Have each student glue the wiggle eyes onto the bumps on the frog's head. Then, have her cut out the tongue pattern, place the pattern on the red felt, and trace. She should cut out the tongue, fold it along the dotted line, and glue it to the mouth opening with the rounded edge facing downward. Finally, have each student draw irregular rounded shapes on the brown felt. Instruct her to glue the spots to the frog's back. After the frog puppets have been completed, ask each student to write a paragraph or story about her frog puppet that is set in Puerto Rico. Each student can share her story using her puppet as a prop.

El gato y el ratón
(The Cat and the Mouse)
Puerto Rican children have played this singing game for hundreds of years.

Ahí viene el gato y el ratón,
a darle combate al tiburón.
Ratón, que te cojo,
que te cojí,
detrás de la mata de ajonjolí.

Have students hold hands in a circle and skip while singing the song continuously. Choose one student to be the mouse and have him stand in the center of the circle. Choose another student to be the cat. The student who is the cat should run around the outside of the circle trying to break in. The students holding hands in the circle should try to keep the cat from sneaking into the circle to tag the mouse. Once the cat comes inside the circle, the mouse should escape from the circle. The cat should try to leave the circle to catch the mouse. Once the mouse has been caught, assign a second pair of students to be the cat and the mouse.

 © Carson-Dellosa • CD-104263

Word Search

Directions: Find the words from the Word Bank in the word search. Words can go across, down, or diagonally.

Word Bank

banana	coquí frog	El Yunque	plena
bomba	Cordillera Central	Mona	San Juan
Cerro de Puenta	Criolla	papaya	Taino
commonwealth	Culebra	plantain	Vieques

```
D  B  L  Q  K  A  M  L  N  D  S  J  C  C  F  J  L  P  P  D
K  Z  A  F  Z  D  K  I  Q  E  H  V  L  E  X  A  U  A  T  D
P  Y  R  N  L  R  A  E  U  W  H  E  V  T  R  J  V  P  G  O
C  E  B  V  A  T  I  Q  O  D  G  K  N  T  U  V  B  A  J  Z
J  O  J  Z  N  N  E  W  Y  I  K  B  N  F  G  S  E  Y  W  L
S  A  M  A  R  I  A  G  C  Q  K  E  J  Y  J  H  V  A  K  P
A  D  L  M  V  D  N  L  D  T  C  V  I  P  J  M  H  X  Y  C
N  P  N  C  O  R  G  C  P  A  T  N  Z  C  L  N  G  S  M  E
J  T  O  X  V  N  U  M  R  R  I  A  T  A  W  C  Y  Q  S  R
U  H  M  U  E  S  W  E  T  N  E  S  P  E  L  O  R  P  O  R
A  T  J  Q  B  T  L  E  U  M  H  W  D  S  I  Q  C  R  K  O
N  U  X  E  O  L  Z  J  A  C  Q  R  N  V  K  U  L  K  X  D
X  A  C  N  I  Q  X  X  H  L  R  S  Y  B  M  Í  E  N  L  E
Q  S  I  D  K  G  M  F  Z  G  T  I  I  M  O  F  C  O  W  P
A  A  R  E  L  Y  U  N  Q  U  E  H  O  Z  N  R  H  R  R  U
T  O  C  U  L  E  B  R  A  P  A  K  Y  L  A  O  P  Q  N  E
C  A  B  M  T  S  C  H  Z  L  L  Z  K  L  L  G  W  N  U  N
P  E  M  N  A  N  A  Q  V  Y  L  E  M  D  R  A  M  B  T  T
T  J  Q  I  S  H  R  R  F  F  V  X  N  X  I  D  E  M  P  A
M  I  X  J  G  N  D  O  I  B  O  M  B  A  M  B  B  H  G  D  W
```

© Carson-Dellosa • CD-104263

The Flag of Puerto Rico

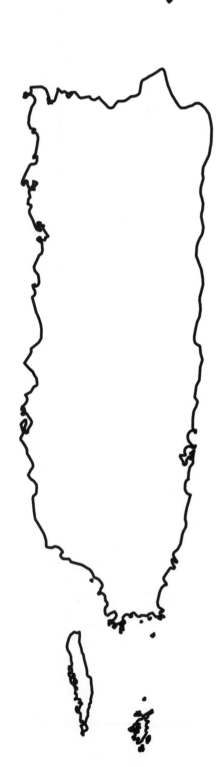

Puerto Rico

14

© Carson-Dellosa · CD-104263

Additional Resources

Books

Brown, Jonatha A. *Puerto Rico and Other Outlying Areas*. Gareth Stevens Publishing, 2005.

Christmas in Puerto Rico (Christmas Around the World). World Book, Inc., 2003.

Fradin, Dennis B. *Puerto Rico*. Children's Press, 1998.

Jaffe, Nina. *The Golden Flower: A Taino Myth from Puerto Rico*. Pinata Books, 2005.

Johnston, Joyce. *Puerto Rico*. Lerner Publishing, 2001.

Kummer, Patricia K. *Puerto Rico*. Capstone Press, Inc., 2002.

Milivojevic, JoAnn. *A Ticket to Puerto Rico*. Carolrhoda Books, 2000.

Ramirez, Michael Rose. *The Legend of the Hummingbird: A Tale from Puerto Rico*. Mondo Publishing, 1998.

Reynolds, Jeff. *Puerto Rico A–Z*. Children's Press, 2005.

Web Sites

CIA World Factbook—Puerto Rico.
https://www.cia.gov/library/publications/the-world-factbook/geos/rq.html

GORP—Caribbean National Forest.
http://gorp.away.com/gorp/resource/us_national_forest/pr_carib.htm

San Juan National Historic Site.
http://www.nps.gov/saju

Welcome to Puerto Rico!
http://Welcome.toPuertoRico.org/index.shtml

World Almanac for Kids—Puerto Rico.
http://www.worldalmanacforkids.com/WAK-Print.aspx?pin=wwwwak-432&chapter_id=15&spanish=

Next Stop: Guatemala

Area: 31,613 sq. miles (108,430 sq. km)
Capital: Guatemala City
Population: 12,728,111
Main Languages: Spanish and Amerindian languages
Main Religion: Roman Catholicism
Currency: Quetzal
Government: Constitutional democratic republic
Flag:

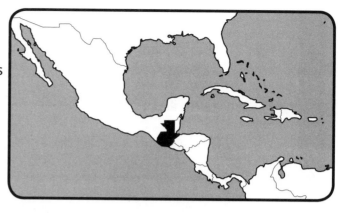

The flag of Guatemala, adopted in 1843, has three vertical stripes of light blue, white, and light blue with a coat of arms centered in the white stripe. The coat of arms includes a green and red quetzal, the national bird, and a scroll with the inscription *Libertad 15 de Septiembre de 1821* (the date of Guatemalan independence from Spain) placed on a pair of crossed rifles and a pair of crossed swords framed by a wreath.

For Your Information

Located in Central America, Guatemala borders the North Pacific Ocean between El Salvador and Mexico. It also borders the Gulf of Honduras between Honduras and Belize. The third largest country in Central America, Guatemala is approximately the same size as the state of Ohio or the country of Ireland. At one time, the capital of Guatemala was the city of Antigua, but an earthquake destroyed the town in 1773. A new capital, Guatemala City, was founded three years later.

The country of Guatemala is known for its high and active volcanoes, for its impressive Mayan ruins, and for its devastating earthquakes. In Guatemala, there are three main geographic regions: highlands, lowlands, and coastal plains. Approximately 60 percent of the population lives in either the coastal plains or the volcanic highlands. Guatemala has some of the world's most beautiful landscapes. Lake Atitlán is located in a volcanic crater and has a depth of 1,000 feet (305 meters), making it the deepest lake in Central America. Because of its beautiful scenery, this lake is one of the most popular tourist destinations in Guatemala.

Even though Guatemala is located in the tropics, its climate varies depending on the elevation and the proximity to the coast. The main advantage of having such a varied climate is that almost every crop that can be grown in the Western Hemisphere can be grown somewhere in Guatemala. Annual rainfall varies from 80 inches (203 centimeters) in the highlands to less than 40 inches (101 centimeters) in the driest areas. The tropical rain forest is Guatemala's most precious resource, with more than 700 varieties of trees and 4,000 types of flowering plants. Some plant species found in Guatemala are not found anywhere else in the world. Recent exploration of Guatemalan rain forests has uncovered treatments for many illnesses and diseases.

Traditional agriculture, which focuses on the production of corn (maize), beans, and squash, is concentrated on small farms in the highlands of Guatemala. Commercial agriculture focuses on the production of coffee, cotton, sugarcane, bananas, and cattle. Guatemala has also become a major world supplier of the spice cardamom.

© Carson-Dellosa • CD-104263

Fascinating Facts

In the rain forest of Guatemala, bird life is colorful and fascinating. A variety of parrots, including the scarlet macaw, make themselves heard and seen. Quetzals, which can grow to more than 4 feet (1.2 meters) in length, share the same habitat as hummingbirds, which are only a few inches in length.

The female villagers of Santiago Atitlán are well-known for their colorful headdresses, which are made from colorful pieces of cloth over 30 feet (9 meters) long. This cloth is continuously coiled around the head to form a halo.

In Petén, American Indians add to their income by climbing sapodilla trees, which can grow to a height of 65 feet (20 meters). After climbing to the tops of the trees, the climbers work their way back down, cutting the bark with their machetes. The sap from the sapodilla tree is collected and sold. The sap contains *chicle*, an ingredient used to make chewing gum.

Armadillos are also found in the rain forest near Petén. The American Indians hunt and kill these armadillos as another source of income. The armadillos are sold to restaurants or cooked and eaten at home.

The writings of the ancient Maya have survived in stone and on four ancient manuscripts. The manuscripts were written on strips of paper called codices made from the pulverized bark of fig trees. These manuscripts measured less than 10 inches (25 centimeters) across, but they were several yards in length. Because of their length, each strip of paper was folded back to back like an accordion fan. These books were covered with jaguar skin.

Arawakan is a family of more than 50 South American languages. Many of these are still spoken in Guatemala today. These languages were once very common and were spoken as far north as Florida and as far south as the border between Argentina and Paraguay. It was the first Amerindian language heard by the Spanish when they arrived in the Americas. We owe the words *canoe*, *tobacco*, and *maize* to the Arawakan languages.

The ruins of Tikal, one of the largest Mayan cities and ceremonial centers, are located in the rain forest of Petén. The center of ancient Tikal is a large plaza which covers approximately two acres (8,094 square meters). To the east is the Temple of the Great Jaguar, named Temple I by archaeologists. This temple contained the tomb of a Tikal ruler whose name translates as "Lord Chocolate." The great temples and pyramids were built without the use of wheels or work animals to help move the huge stone blocks, some weighing as much as 60 tons (54 metric tons).

For most people in Guatemala, tortillas are considered "the bread of life." Tortillas are thin, round pancakes made from corn or flour. No meal is complete without this bread. Tortillas are usually topped with beans and vegetables and seasoned with chili salsa. A large variety of chilies is available in Guatemala. Chilies are used to make various sauces and spices. Usually, the longer chilies are cooked, the stronger they taste.

© Carson-Dellosa • CD-104263

Spanish Language Activities

Everyday Expressions

hola	hello
adiós	good-bye
por favor	please
gracias	thank you
Mi nombre es . . .	My name is . . .
¿Que tál?	How are you?
No te preocupes.	Don't worry.
Ven aquí.	Come here.
¿Te puedo ayudar?	Can I help?

Animals

el caimán	alligator
el ave	bird
la mariposa	butterfly
el gato	cat
el pollo	chicken
la vaca	cow
el perro	dog
el pez	fish
la rana	frog
el caballo	horse
el cerdo	pig
el gallo	rooster

School Life

el profesor	teacher
el alumno	pupil
el aula	classroom
la biblioteca	library
el comedor	dining hall
el gimnasio	gym
el encerado	blackboard
la tiza	chalk
un libro	book
el lápiz	pencil
el papel	paper
un libro de apuntes	notebook

Guatemalan Poem

Un pájaro blanco con el cuello largo	A long necked white bird watches
Curiosamente ve el lago azul	Curiously at the blue lake
Que cubre la isla de Flores en Petén	Surrounding Flores island in Petén
Pensando que un pez aparezca	Thinking a fish might appear
Y le haga su día.	And make his day.
Yo también veo el mismo lago	I am looking at the same lake
Admiro la grandiosa belleza	Admiring its wide expanse of beauty
Que besa el cielo azul	That kisses the blue sky
Y manda olas a la orilla.	And sends ripples to the shore.
–Author Unknown	–Translated by Cesar Macedo

© Carson-Dellosa • CD-104263

Recipes

Tortillas

Ingredients:
2 cups (473 mL) *masa barina* (corn meal
    may be substituted)
1 cup (237 mL) water
1 tsp. (5 mL) salt

Directions:
Mix and stir the *masa barina* (corn mixed with lime water ground into a fine meal), water, and salt in a bowl. Gently knead by hand until the dough is firm and does not fall apart in your hands. Shape the dough into 12 balls of the same size and place each ball into a tortilla press. (If a tortilla press is not available, use a rolling pin to flatten each ball.) Flatten each ball to approximately ¼" (0.64 cm) thickness. Fry on medium heat on each side for approximately one minute. Yield: 12 tortillas

Licuado de Sandía
(Fruit Smoothie)

Ingredients:
2 cups (473 mL) crushed ice
1 cup (237 mL) fresh sliced watermelon,
    mango, or strawberries, cut into pieces
⅔ cup (142 mL) water
¼ cup (59 mL) sugar

Directions:
Put ice, fruit, water, and sugar into a blender. Cover and blend until smooth. Yield: 6 servings

Arroz Guatemalteco
(Guatemalan-Style Rice)

Ingredients:
2 tbsp. (30 mL) vegetable oil
1 onion, finely chopped
3 cloves garlic, chopped
1 green pepper, finely chopped
2 carrots, finely chopped
1 cup (237 mL) uncooked rice
2½ cups (592.5 mL) water
½ cup (118 mL) green peas
salt
pepper

Directions:
Heat oil in skillet over medium-high heat. Add the onion and garlic and cook until soft (approximately three minutes). Add rice, green pepper, and carrots, stirring continuously for approximately three minutes. Add water and bring to a boil. Cover, reduce heat, and simmer for 20 minutes or until the water is absorbed and the rice is tender. Add the peas. Season with salt and pepper to taste. Yield: 4–6 servings

Classroom Activities

Designing a Guatemalan Plate

Materials:
paper plates
markers
yarn
paint
paintbrushes
pencils
hole punch
scissors

Directions:
1. Have each student draw a design on a paper plate similar to one shown above, or have him use one of the following suggestions: a sun, a jaguar, a hummingbird, or a parrot.
2. Then, instruct each student to add an attractive, colorful border around the edges of his paper plate.
3. Allow each student to paint or color his design as he wishes.
4. Next, tell each student to use a hole punch to punch a hole in the top of the plate.
5. Finally, cut a piece of colorful yarn for each student to hang his plate.

Making a Guatemalan Mask

Today in Guatemala, masks are often used in traditional dances, ceremonies, and pageants.

Materials:
paper plates
craft sticks
markers, tempera paint,
    or crayons
pencils
yarn
fabric scraps
glitter
glue or glue stick
stapler or tape
scissors
hole punch

Directions:
Have each student punch two eye holes in her paper plate with the hole punch (see diagram at right). Next, each student should staple or tape a craft stick to the bottom of the plate and turn the plate over. Have her draw a design of a person or animal using markers, tempera paint, or crayons. To enhance the mask, have each student add scraps of fabric, glitter, or yarn. Ask students to share their masks with the class.

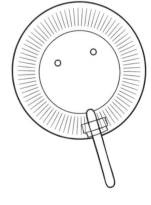

© Carson-Dellosa • CD-104263

Classroom Activities

Ruby-Throated Hummingbirds

Dozens of hummingbird species are found in the tropical rain forest near Petén, Guatemala. One species, the ruby-throated hummingbird, spends winters in Guatemala and migrates thousands of miles to the United States in the spring to breed. These tiny birds can fly forward or hover in midair. They are called hummingbirds because of the humming sound their wings often make. Their wings beat approximately 55–75 times each second. A hummingbird's feet and legs are so tiny that they cannot walk or even hop. They mostly use their feet and legs for perching. Their diets consist of tiny bugs and nectar from flowers. Hummingbirds use their long tongues to drink nectar. These colorful birds make their nests from spider webs, lichens, and the fluffy seed coverings of plants.

- -

Name _____

Ruby-Throated Hummingbirds

Directions: Use crayons or markers to color the hummingbirds according to the descriptions.

Adult male: green head and back, ruby-red throat, gray sides, tail has no white
Adult female: green head and back, white chest and throat, tail has white tips

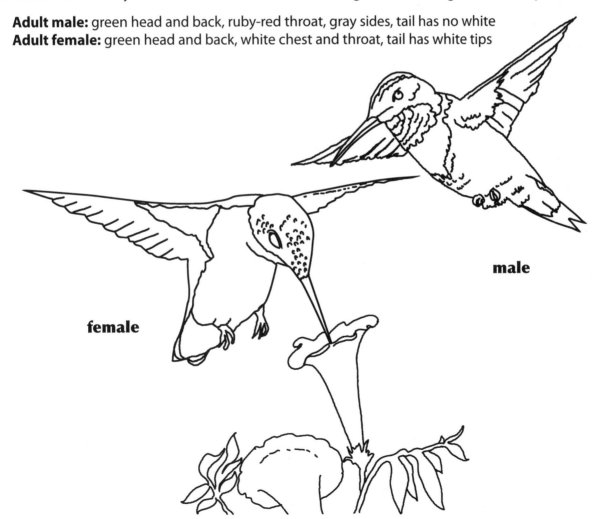

male

female

© Carson-Dellosa • CD-104263

Crossword Puzzle

Directions: Complete the crossword puzzle using the clues.

Across:
3. a word that means "hello" in Spanish
4. an area of Guatemala where a rain forest is found
6. an ingredient from tree sap that is used to make chewing gum
7. a plant that is used to spice various foods
8. a type of parrot found in Guatemala
10. an animal that hunters catch in the rain forest and sell to restaurants
11. a family of South American languages
12. the capital city of Guatemala
13. a grain similar to corn

Down:
1. a food known as "the bread of life" in Guatemala
2. type of currency used in Guatemala
5. ancient Mayan ruins
8. a type of tree whose sap is used to make gum
9. items worn during traditional dances and ceremonies

© Carson-Dellosa • CD-104263

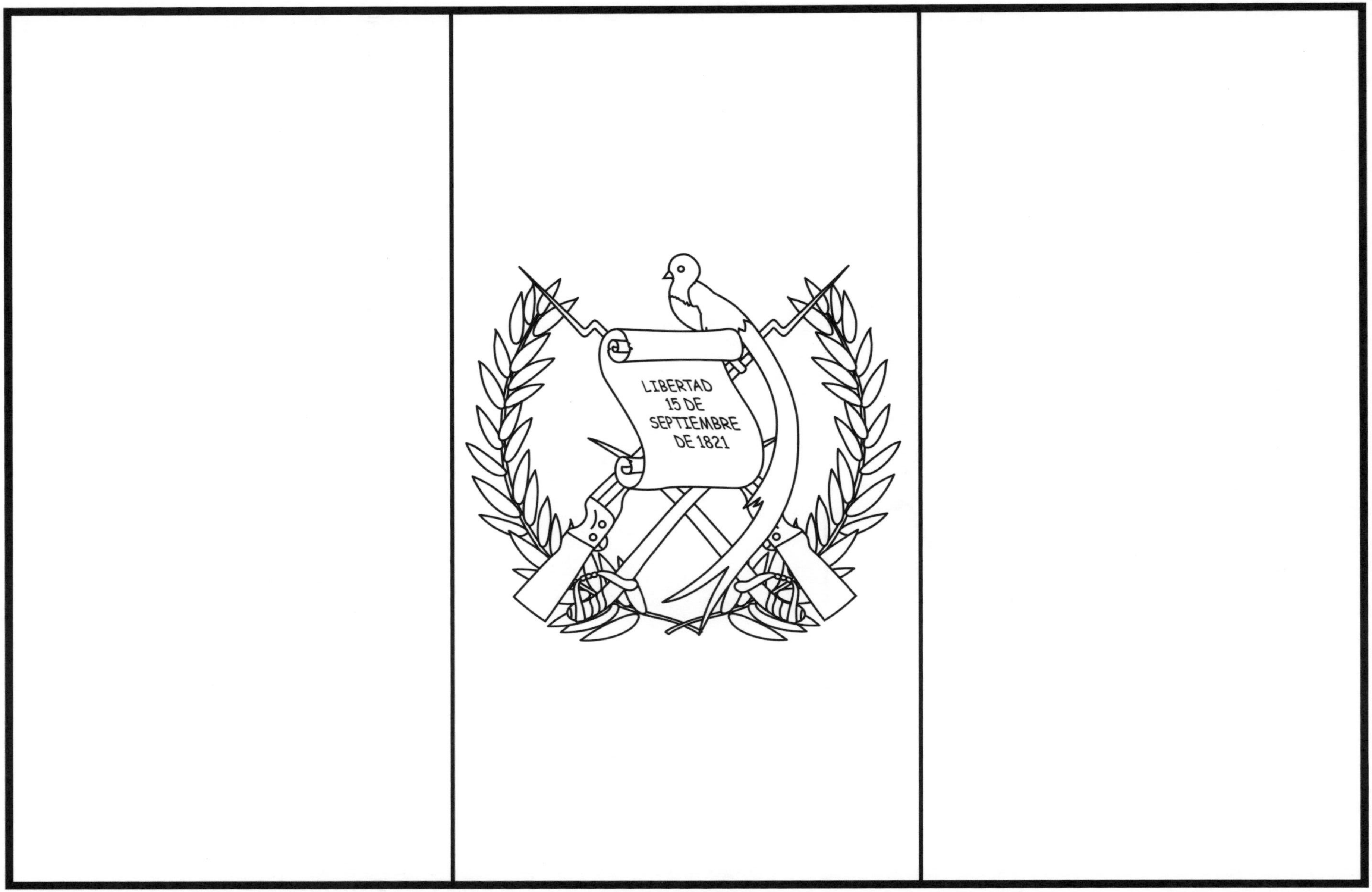
LIBERTAD
15 DE
SEPTIEMBRE
DE 1821

The Flag of Guatemala

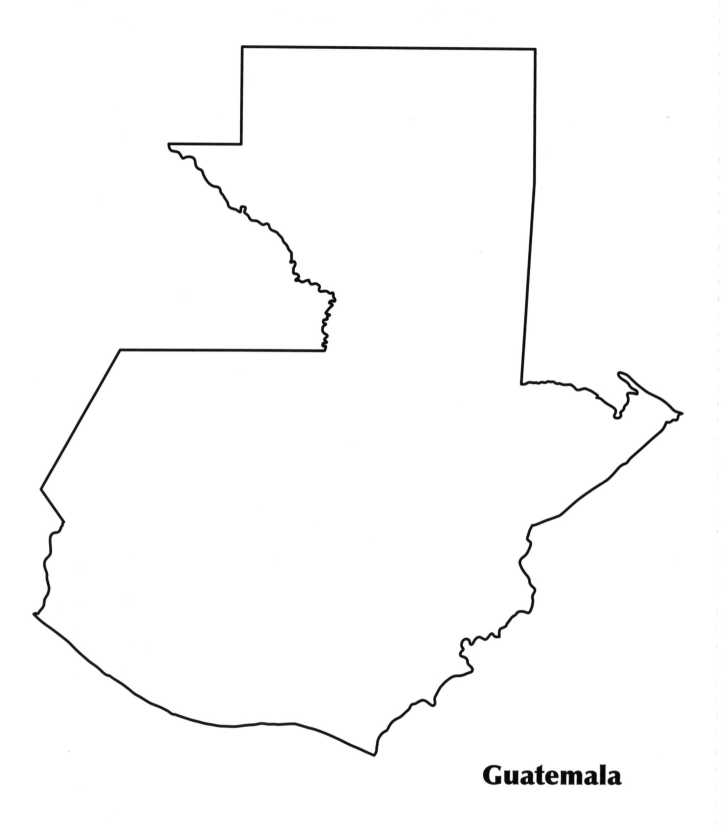

Guatemala

© Carson-Dellosa • CD-104263

Additional Resources

Books

Aboff, Marcie. *Guatemala ABC's: A Book About the People and Places of Guatemala*. Picture Window Books, 2003.

Braman, Arlette N. *Kids Around the World Create!* Jossey-Bass Publishers, 1999.

Brill, Marlene Targ. *Journey for Peace: The Story of Rigoberta Menchu*. Dutton Juvenile, 1996.

Cameron, Ann. *The Most Beautiful Place in the World*. Yearling Books, 1993.

Castaneda, Omar S. *Abuela's Weave*. Lee & Low Books, 1993.

Morrison, Marion. *World in View: Central America*. Raintree Books, 1993.

Noble, John. *Lonely Planet: Guatemala*. Lonely Planet Publications, 2004.

O'Kane, Trish. *Guatemala: A Guide to the People, Politics, and Culture* (*In Focus* series). Latin America Bureau, 1999.

Parker, Edward. *Country Fact Files: Central America*. Raintree Publishers, 1999.

Sheehan, Sean. *Cultures of the World: Guatemala*. Marshall Cavendish Corporation, 1998.

Simons, Suzanne. *Trouble Dolls: A Guatemalan Legend*. Apple Publishing, 2000.

Terzian, Alexandra. *The Kids' Multicultural Art Book*. Williamson Books, 1993.

Wisniewski, David. *Rain Player*. Clarion Books, 1996.

Wolf, Eric. *Sons of the Shaking Earth*. University of Chicago Press, 1962.

Web Sites

CIA World Factbook—Guatemala.
https://www.cia.gov/library/publications/the-world-factbook/geos/gt.html

Enjoy Guatemala.
http://www.enjoyguatemala.com/culture.htm

Guatemala Facts.
http://larutamayaonline.com/guatemala_facts.php

National Geographic—Guatemala.
http://www3.nationalgeographic.com/places/countries/country_guatemala.html

Arriving in Cuba

Area: 42,803 sq. miles (110,861 sq. km)
Capital City: Havana
Population: 11,394,043
Main Language: Spanish
Main Religion: Roman Catholicism
Currency: Cuban peso
Government: Communist state
Flag:

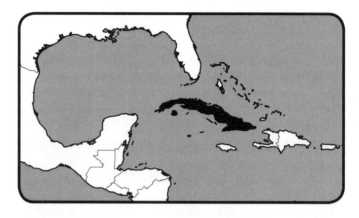

The Cuban flag was adopted in 1902. It has five equal horizontal bands alternating between blue and white with the top and bottom bands being blue. On the hoist side (the side of the flag that is attached to a flagpole or staff), there is a single white star in a red triangle, which symbolizes equality.

For Your Information

The country of Cuba, officially known as the Republic of Cuba, is the largest island in the West Indies. Cuba consists of more than 1,600 smaller islands along with the large main island. Located between the Atlantic Ocean and the Caribbean Sea, Cuba is 90 miles (145 kilometers) south of the state of Florida.

Cuba, which is slightly smaller than the state of Pennsylvania, has a coastline of 2,100 miles (3,380 kilometers). Almost three-fourths of the main island consists of low-lying large plains and river basins. The Sierra Maestra Mountains are in the east, with a peak elevation of 6,542 feet (1,944 meters). The longest river is the Cauto River, which is 155 miles (249 kilometers) long. On the western end of Cuba are numerous caves, including the largest of all: the Great Cavern of Santo Tomás. This huge cave has more than 27 miles (44 kilometers) of passages. The cave entrance leads into a maze of six levels with more than 50 separate caves.

Because of its tropical climate, seasonal rainfall, and low-lying land, Cuba's economy is largely focused on agriculture. The average annual temperature is 75°F (24°C). It has only two clear seasons during the year—the wet season and the dry season. Cuban agriculture is slowly diversifying despite the tropical climate. Most of Cuba's flat or forested areas are now used for growing tobacco, coffee, or sugar on large plantations. Other crops include rice, citrus fruits, potatoes, plantains, corn, bananas, and cassavas. Cattle, pigs, and chickens are common livestock. Fishing resources include tuna, hake, and needlefish.

Tourism is now the fastest growing industry in Cuba. Tourists from all over the world visit Cuba to see white sand beaches, historic buildings, and interesting nightlife. During recent years, great effort has been made to modernize and increase the tourism business. Many new hotels and resorts were built by Spanish and Canadian investors.

© Carson-Dellosa • CD-104263

Fascinating Facts

 Baseball is Cuba's national sport. The Cuban National Baseball Team is one of the best in the world, and they have the Olympic gold medals to prove it. Since there are no professional sports leagues in Cuba, players often leave for the United States to play professionally and to earn more money.

 In a communist state, the people work for the good of the community and not for individual profit. In Cuba, laborers earn almost as much as professionals. For example, a taxi driver may earn as much as or more money than a doctor. Farmers, miners, factory workers, and fishermen make up much of the work force.

 Cuba is famous for its wide variety of animal species, including flamingos, tarantulas, sharks, bats, and iguanas. Some of Cuba's rarest animals live in the *Ciénega de Zapata* (Zapata Swamp). Among the animals living in the Zapata Swamp are the 10-foot-long (3 meters) alligator gar, one of the largest freshwater fish in the world, and the *jutía* (tree rat).

 During their leisure time, Cubans play a variety of games. Dominoes and chess are especially popular with teenagers and adults. Children prefer playing marbles and *Chocolonga*, a game similar to Pin the Tail on the Donkey. In order to play the game, a blindfolded person is turned around three or four times and then must find the exact center of a circle on a wall or other surface.

 The national tree of Cuba is the royal palm, which can grow as tall as 60 feet (18 meters) high. The botanical name for the palm tree is *Roystonea*, named for General Roy Stone of the United States. Tens of thousands of these trees can be found in Cuba.

 A wide variety of music is produced in Cuba, including rock, folk, classical, country, and *salsa*, a rhythmic dance music with complicated harmonies. Salsa music can be heard at restaurants, public clubs, neighborhood parties, and music festivals. The biggest influence on salsa music is the traditional *son*, originally from Africa, which features complicated rhythms, overlapping beats, and "call and response" vocals.

 Spanish and Caribbean cuisines combine to form Cuban cuisine. Cuban foods use spices from the Caribbean along with Spanish cooking techniques. A traditional meal, which is served with all food items placed on the table at the same time, consists of black beans and rice, plantains, *ropa vieja* (a shredded beef dish whose name actually means "old clothes"), Cuban bread, pork with onions, and tropical fruits.

 Cuban children attend primary school from ages 5 to 11 and secondary school until they are 17 years old. Primary-level students wear red and white uniforms and secondary-level students wear yellow and white uniforms. Students who are obviously talented in sports can attend special sports schools to receive their education.

Spanish Language Activities

Common Cuban Expressions

Hay/No hay . . .	There is/There is not . . .
¿Cuánto cuesta?	What does it cost?
¿Dónde está . . . ?	Where is . . . ?
Me gustaría . . .	I would like . . .
Mucho gusto.	I am pleased to meet you.
Hablo muy poco español.	I speak very little Spanish.
buenos días	good day

Guantanamera

This song is probably the best known and most patriotic Cuban song.
The lyrics are based on a poem by José Martí.

Yo soy un hombre sincero	I am a truthful man
De donde crece la palma.	From where the palm tree grows.
Y antes de morirme quiero	And before dying I want
Echar mis versos del alma.	To let out the verses of my soul.
Guantanamera, guajira, Guantanamera.	*Guantanamera, guajira, Guantanamera.*
Mi verso es de un verde claro	My verse is light green
Y de un carmín encendido.	And it is flaming red.
Mi verso es un ciervo herido	My verse is a wounded stag
Que busca en el monte amparo.	Who seeks refuge on the mountain.
Guantanamera, guajira, Guantanamera.	*Guantanamera, guajira, Guantanamera.*
Con los pobres de la tierra	With the poor people of the earth
Quiero yo mi suerte echar.	I want to cast my lot.
El arroyo de la sierra	The brook of the mountains
Me complace más que el mar.	Gives me more pleasure than the sea.
Guantanamera, guajira, Guantanamera.	*Guantanamera, guajira, Guantanamera.*

 © Carson-Dellosa • CD-104263

Recipes

Fríjoles Negros
(Black Beans)

Ingredients:
20 oz. (591 mL) canned black beans
1 green pepper
1 red pepper
1 onion
4 garlic cloves
1 tsp. (5 mL) cumin powder
½ tsp. (2.5 mL) ground oregano
½ tsp. (2.5 mL) salt
¼ tsp. (1.25 mL) black pepper
1 tbsp. (15 mL) white vinegar

Directions:
As you heat the beans on a stove top, finely chop the green and red peppers, onions, and garlic cloves. Sauté the onions, peppers, and garlic. Add cumin, salt, black pepper, and oregano and let the ingredients simmer for 15–30 minutes. Mix the sautéed ingredients with the beans and add vinegar. Reheat to serve.
Yield: 6 servings

Tostones
(Fried Plantains)

Ingredients:
4 average-sized green plantains
2 oz. (59 mL) salt
2 cups (473 mL) cooking oil

Directions:
Peel the plantains and remove the ends. Cut each plantain into 1"-thick (2.5 cm) pieces. Deep fry plantains in oil until brown on each side. Remove plantains from oil and place on a paper towel to drain grease. Smash each piece into a pancake. Deep fry plantain pancakes in oil again for three minutes. Remove from oil, place on paper towel, and add salt. Yield: 6 servings

Arroz Blanco
(White Rice)

Ingredients:
4 cups (946 mL) white rice
12 cups (2.8 L) water
1 oz. (30 mL) salt
4 garlic cloves
2 oz. (59 mL) cooking oil

Directions:
Wash and rinse rice grains. Peel the garlic. Heat the oil on low-medium heat in a large saucepan and add garlic cloves. Once the garlic is golden brown, remove it from the oil. Add water and salt to the oil. Bring to a boil by increasing the heat, then add the rice. Lower the heat and simmer for 30 minutes.

Fritas
(Cuban Hamburger)

Ingredients:
1½ lb (0.68 kg) ground beef
¼ cup (59 mL) milk
½ cup (118 mL) ground bread crumbs
4 oz. (118 mL) onions
1 large egg
⅛ cup (30 mL) ketchup
2 tsp. (10 mL) salt
1 oz. fresh green pepper
1 tsp. (5 mL) Worcestershire sauce
1 tsp. (5 mL) black pepper
6 small hamburger buns

Directions:
Finely mince the onion and green pepper. Place the ground beef into a large mixing bowl. Add all of the ingredients except the bread crumbs and the hamburger buns. Mix thoroughly. Slowly add bread crumbs until the mixture is firm. Shape into six balls and flatten into hamburger patties. Grill or fry hamburgers on lightly greased pan. Yield: 6 servings

Classroom Activities

1. Cuba's flag is fun to paint! Place the following in a classroom center: large sheets of white construction paper, blue and red tempera paint, and paintbrushes. Have students copy the flag from a book or from the full-page reproducible (page 34) and then paint it. When dry, students can write facts about Cuba on the backs of their flags. Display the colorful flags around the classroom or in a hallway.

2. Baseball is the national sport of Cuba. Have students research famous Cuban baseball players and report their findings to the class. Or, play baseball (or softball) with the class during recess or physical education.

3. Cubans listen to and dance to salsa music throughout the year. Invite a local dance group or dance teacher to introduce students to salsa. Students can also create their own movements to the music.

4. Have students work in cooperative groups to compare their state, region, or country to Cuba. Students can research information about the average weather conditions, city sizes, population, area, geography, popular sports, etc. Have groups present the information to the class as if they are travel agents preparing a trip to Cuba.

5. Play Spanish Bingo! Make one copy of the BINGO card (page 31) for each student. Write one Spanish word from the list below in each square of each BINGO card. Make sure that each card is different. Give each student a copy of the Bingo Words list below. Call out the words in English. Players should cover the squares with the Spanish equivalents with playing chips until one person covers a row of squares (horizontally, vertically, or diagonally) and calls out "BINGO!"

Bingo Words

hola	hello	*mamá*	mother	*uno*	one
sí	yes	*papá*	father	*dos*	two
no	no	*buenos días*	good day	*tres*	three
amigo	friend	*lunes*	Monday	*cuatro*	four
muy bien	very good	*martes*	Tuesday	*cinco*	five
por favor	please	*miércoles*	Wednesday	*seis*	six
gracias	thank you	*jueves*	Thursday	*siete*	seven
mí	me	*viernes*	Friday	*ocho*	eight
tu	you	*sábado*	Saturday	*nueve*	nine
aquí	here	*domingo*	Sunday	*diez*	ten

© Carson-Dellosa • CD-104263

B I N G O

		GRATIS		

Map Activity

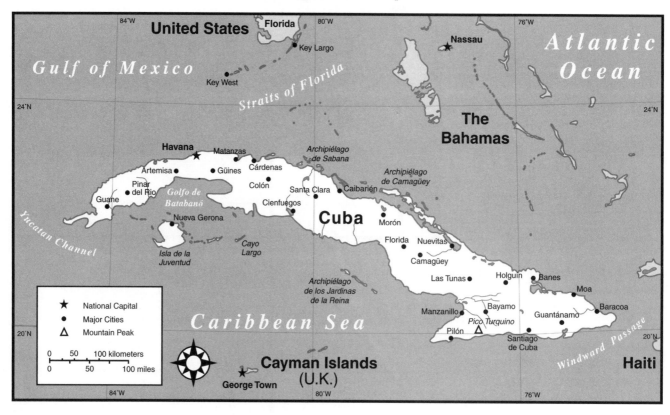

Directions: Use the map to answer the questions.

1. The _____ is the body of water located south of Cuba.
   A. Gulf of Mexico   B. Caribbean Sea   C. Atlantic Ocean   D. Cayman Islands

2. Pico Turquino is a _____.
   A. major city   B. capital   C. mountain peak   D. naval base

3. The distance between Pinar del Rio and Havana is about _____ miles.
   A. 50   B. 25   C. 75   D. 100

4. _____ is the capital city of Cuba.
   A. Guantánamo   B. Matanzas   C. Pico Turquino   D. Havana

5. The distance between the city of Manzanillo and the city of Bayamo is about _____.
   A. 50 kilometers   B. 50 miles   C. 100 kilometers   D. 100 miles

6. Bayamo is closest to the city of _____.
   A. Guantánamo   B. Havana   C. Santiago de Cuba   D. Holguín

                                    © Carson-Dellosa • CD-104263

Name _____

Word Search

Directions: Find the words from the Word Bank in the word search. Words can go across, down, or diagonally.

Word Bank

baseball	Great Cavern	rice	sports schools
black beans	Guantanamera	royal palm	Zapata Swamp
Caribbean Sea	Havana	Santiago de Cuba	
dominoes	Pico Turquino	son	

```
P  Z  C  W  N  W  C  C  A  R  S  I  P  L  L
I  A  A  N  X  E  V  N  C  T  A  W  U  G  A
C  P  R  C  R  M  A  B  B  X  N  B  Y  R  D
O  A  I  A  I  V  P  L  L  T  T  V  E  E  O
T  T  B  C  A  R  I  C  E  O  I  M  I  A  M
U  A  B  H  N  X  Z  V  D  S  A  E  X  T  I
R  S  E  Y  C  L  E  B  N  N  G  T  B  C  N
Q  W  A  G  Y  N  L  A  A  T  O  O  J  A  O
U  A  N  P  D  T  E  T  U  S  D  Y  C  V  E
I  M  S  T  M  B  N  K  O  R  E  L  O  E  S
N  P  E  R  K  A  N  W  S  F  C  B  O  R  N
O  K  A  C  U  S  R  B  O  W  U  J  A  N  B
C  O  A  G  R  V  D  F  N  E  B  S  S  L  S
X  L  U  F  R  O  Y  A  L  P  A  L  M  J  L
B  R  S  P  O  R  T  S  S  C  H  O  O  L  S
```

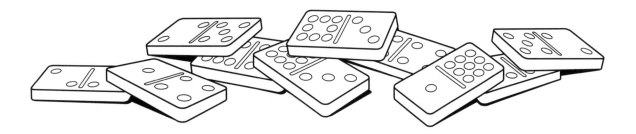

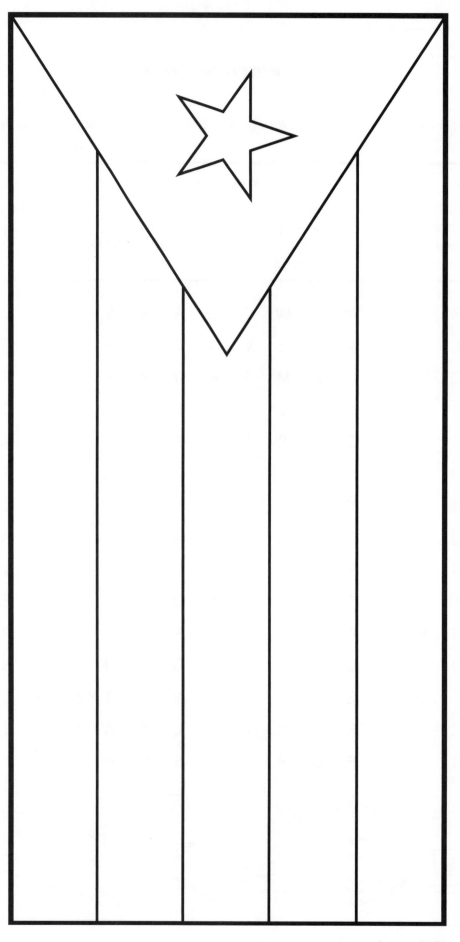

The Flag of Cuba

34

© Carson-Dellosa • CD-104263

Cuba

© Carson-Dellosa • CD-104263

Additional Resources

Books

Ada, Alma Flor. *Under the Royal Palms: A Childhood in Cuba*. Atheneum, 1998.

Crouch, Clifford W. *Cuba*. Chelsea House, 1997.

Crouch, Clifford W. *Places and Peoples of the World: Cuba*. Chelsea House, 1991.

Cramer, Mark. *Countries of the World: Cuba*. Gareth Stevens Publishing, 2000.

Cramer, Mark. *Culture Shock! Cuba*. Graphic Arts Center, 1998.

Fox, Mary Virginia. *Modern Nations of the World: Cuba*. Lucent Books, 1998.

Haverstock, Nathan A. *Cuba in Pictures*. Lerner Publishing, 1997.

Mara, William P. *Countries of the World: Cuba*. Bridgestone Books, 1999.

Roque, Ismael. *Cuba for Kids*. Cuba for Kids Foundation, 2000.

Santella, Andrew. *Roosevelt's Rough Riders*. Compass Point Books, 2006.

Sheehan, Sean. *Cultures of the World: Cuba*. Benchmark Books, 1994.

Web Sites

CIA World Factbook—Cuba.
https://www.cia.gov/library/publications/the-world-factbook/geos/cu.html

The Cuban Experience.
http://library.thinkquest.org/18355/

Lonely Planet—Cuba.
http://www.lonelyplanet.com/destinations/caribbean/cuba

National Geographic—Cuba.
http://www3.nationalgeographic.com/places/countries/country_cuba.html

Official Site of the Republic of Cuba.
http://www.cubagob.cu/ingles/default.htm

 © Carson-Dellosa • CD-104263

On to Peru

Area: 494,211 sq. miles (1,280,000 sq. km)
Capital City: Lima
Population: 28,674,757
Main Languages: Spanish, Quechua, and Aymara
Main Religion: Roman Catholicism
Currency: Nuevo sol
Government: Constitutional republic
Flag:

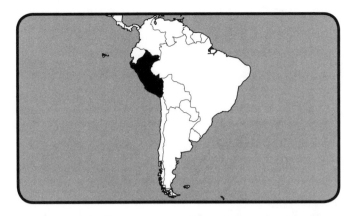

The flag of Peru, which was adopted in 1825, has three equal, vertical bands of red, white, and red. The coat of arms is in the middle band and contains pictures of a shield with a vicuña (a llama-like animal), a cinchona tree, and a yellow cornucopia full of gold coins. The shield is surrounded by a green laurel wreath and branches with red berries and ribbons.

For Your Information

Peru, the third largest country in South America, borders Ecuador and Columbia to the north and the Pacific Ocean to the west. The country contains three geographic regions: the coast, the mountains, and the rain forest. The coast is a narrow, low-lying desert region that stretches 1,448 miles (2,330 kilometers) along the Pacific Ocean. The Peruvian desert receives less than one cup (237 milliliters) of measurable precipitation every two years, making it one of the driest deserts on Earth. The Andes Mountains are made up of two parallel ranges that run the length of Peru and separate the coast from the rain forest. The tropical rain forest of the Amazon River basin lies to the east of the Andes. This rain forest, combined with the slopes of the Andes, covers 62 percent of Peru.

Each of the three geographic regions has its own climate and weather pattern. On the coast, the dry season lasts from December until April, with temperatures ranging between 85°–95°F (29°–35°C). In the mountains, the dry season lasts from May until September. The mountains receive large amounts of rainfall between October and April. In the rain forest, the wet season lasts from January until April. Heavy rains often cause landslides.

One of Peru's main industries is mining. Copper mines employ the majority of the labor force. Other important products and industries include petroleum, chemicals, building materials, electronic products, food processing, pharmaceuticals, plastic products, and textiles. Agricultural crops include rice, sugarcane, corn, and cotton. The main agricultural export is coffee.

Native people make up the largest part of the Peruvian population. The two largest native groups are the Aymara, who live in the southeast, and the Quechua, who live throughout the country but mainly in the mountains. The next largest population group is the *mestizos*, whose ancestors are both native Peruvians and Europeans. The remaining population consists of Africans, Japanese, Chinese, and other groups.

Fascinating Facts

 Lamoids, relatives of the camel family, roam throughout the Andes Mountains. The first Europeans called them "Peruvian sheep." Settlers domesticated these animals, and people have been using their wool and meat ever since. Members of the lamoid family include llamas, alpacas, vicuñas, and guanacos. These animals serve as pack animals for Peruvians.

 The famous Inca city of Machu Picchu is in Peru. Many people believe it is the most amazing archaeological site in the Americas. Often called the "forgotten city," Machu Picchu is one of the last remnants of the great Inca empire. Thousands of tourists travel to these ruins every year. The city was deserted sometime before the Spanish conquest in 1532.

 The ancient Nazca civilization is best known for the lines and drawings of animals (including a spider, a monkey, a whale, and birds) that cover a large area of the desert around their valley. These lines were created by removing dark stones to expose the lighter, sandy ground underneath. The lines are best seen from a hill or from the air.

 In the 19th century, steamships were brought to Peru from England. They were disassembled, and mules carried the pieces to the shore of Lake Titicaca, which is 12,507 feet (3,812 meters) above sea level. The ships were then reassembled to carry passengers and cargo across the lake between the countries of Bolivia and Peru. The oldest of these ships, the *Yavari*, was launched on Christmas Day in 1870. At that time, the steam engine was fueled by enormous quantities of dried llama dung, the most plentiful fuel in the area.

 The haircutting ceremony is a Peruvian tradition that was passed down from the Inca civilization. This ceremony is still followed in parts of the mountain regions. A child's first haircutting is attended by friends and family and is called the *rutuchicoy*. The child's parents provide food and drinks. Each adult may cut a lock of hair and present the child with a gift, usually a small sum of money, which is put aside for later years.

 The potato (which originated in the Andes where there are more than 150 varieties) can be yellow, white, purple, or red and comes in all shapes and sizes. The mountain people have devised a way of preserving potatoes. They spread the potatoes outside on the ground and stomp on them to squeeze out the water. The potatoes are then left outside for several days in the hot sun and in the freezing night temperatures. In its dehydrated state, the potato is known as a *chuño*.

 A wide variety of plant life in the jungles of Peru has led to many important discoveries in the creation of medicines. Some of these medicines include aspirin, quinine (a drug for malaria), curare (a muscle relaxant), and medications used in the treatment of cancer. These discoveries are relatively new to the outside world, but rain forest tribes have used these medicinal plants for many years.

© Carson-Dellosa • CD-104263

Spanish Language Activities

Peruvian Expressions

¿Y qué tal cómo va?	And how is it going?
No pasa nada.	Nothing happens.
Nada que ver.	Nothing to see.
¿Qué pasa?	What's up?
¿Cuánto cuesta la carrera?	How much is the taxi?
¿Tienes una máquina?	Do you have a computer (in a cyber café)?
Me encanta este vestido.	I love this dress.
Me empujé un calderón de gallardo.	I ate chicken soup.
¡Suave!	Take it easy!
¡Qué palta!	I was so embarrassed.

Spanish and Quechua are the official languages of Peru. Here are some common expressions in Spanish, Quechua, and English.

Spanish	Quechua	English
¿Cuántos años tienes?	*Jaiq'a watayoq kanki?*	How old are you?
¿Dónde vives?	*Maypin tiyanki?*	Where do you live?
Estoy enfermo.	*Onq'osianin.*	I am sick.
¿De dónde es usted, señor?	*Maymantataq kanki taytay?*	Where do you come from, sir?
Yo soy de los Estados Unidos.	*Estados Unidosmantan kani.*	I'm from the United States.

Peruvian Children's Song
Composed by H. Ludovico M.

Batallón Infantil

Viva la Patria, Viva el Perú,
Viva la Escuela y su Juventud.
Este batallón es de los valientes,
Que en la Escuela son los mas chiquitines,
Mas ya su valor viene a demostrar,
Que son la esperanza de nuestra Nación.

Battalion Child

Long live the Mother Country, long live Peru.
Long live the schools and their youth.
This battle song is for the brave,
Those who are the smallest ones in school,
Their courage is already demonstrated,
for they are the hopes of our nation.

Recipe

Peruvian Causa
(Layered Chilled Potato Salad)

Potatoes

Ingredients:
2 large yellow potatoes
2 large blue potatoes (use another variety if needed)
2 large white potatoes
½ tsp. (3 mL) saffron
4½ tbsp. (67 mL) butter or margarine
sea salt

Directions:
Keeping each type of potato separate, peel all of the potatoes and cut them into small pieces. Boil each type of potato in a separate pot. Add saffron to the yellow potatoes. Cook all of the potatoes until tender (approximately 20 minutes). Drain the potatoes and mash each type separately, adding the butter or margarine and sea salt (to taste) to each. Set aside.

Olive Mixture

Ingredients:
⅓ cup (79 mL) kalamata olives
⅓ cup (79 mL) green olives
3 cloves garlic
1½ tbsp. (22 mL) capers
2 tbsp. (30 mL) parsley
1 medium roasted red bell pepper
1 tsp. (5 mL) olive oil
juice of 1 lemon

Directions:
Finely chop the olives, parsley, and red pepper. Mince the capers and garlic. Combine all of the ingredients in a bowl.

Final Preparations

Line a loaf pan with plastic wrap. The plastic wrap should extend over the edges of the pan. Layer one variety of mashed potatoes in the bottom of the pan and spread evenly. Spread half of the olive mixture on top of the potato layer. Add another potato layer followed by the rest of the olive mixture. Finish with the third potato layer. Fold the plastic wrap to cover the top and chill in the refrigerator overnight. The next day, slice and serve. If possible, serve with Huancaina sauce, a creamy Peruvian cheese sauce.

 © Carson-Dellosa • CD-104263

Classroom Activities

Materials:
postcard pattern (below)
pen
markers
card stock
scissors
glue
clear contact paper
hole punch
yarn
library books and Web sites about
    Peru (see page 45)

Directions:
1. Have each student research facts about Peru.
2. On a copy of the postcard pattern, have each student write a short note to a friend or relative describing a tourist attraction in Peru.
3. In the blank box in the upper right corner of the postcard pattern, have each student design a stamp that represents a different attraction in Peru.
4. Have each student address her postcard to a friend or relative.
5. Next, have each student cut out the postcard pattern, glue it to a piece of card stock, and cut the card stock to the postcard's size.
6. Tell each student to draw a colorful picture of the tourist attraction described in the message on the front of the postcard.
7. Cover the picture side of each postcard with clear contact paper. Punch a hole in the top of each postcard and string a piece of yarn through the hole for hanging.
8. Display students' postcards in the classroom.

Name _____

Word Search

Directions: Find the words from the Word Bank in the word search. Words can go across, down, or diagonally.

Word Bank

Andes	Lake Titicaca	Nazca
Aymara	lamoids	potato
causa	Lima	Quechua
chuño	llama	rutuchicoy
coffee	Machu Picchu	Spanish
copper	mestizo	vicuña

M A C H U P I C C H U X Q A B

S N L T L X C R M E S T I Z O

M P V N E U O U X U D V K L N

C M A J L A P T S X Q I L D G

Q X W N R C P U G C B C A H U

H L Q A I G E C C A T U K P B

K N M C T S R H C U O Ñ E O D

F Y Q B Q U H I H S J A T T G

A X U R K U C C U A C G I A C

S F E O P J A O Ñ L N H T T O

A A C P H O F Y O K I A I O F

W N H G L A M O I D S M C F F

X D U A P M D U L L A M A E E

L E A O K X U D B I C L C Z E

X S U Z M J F P N A Z C A M L

42

© Carson-Dellosa • CD-104263

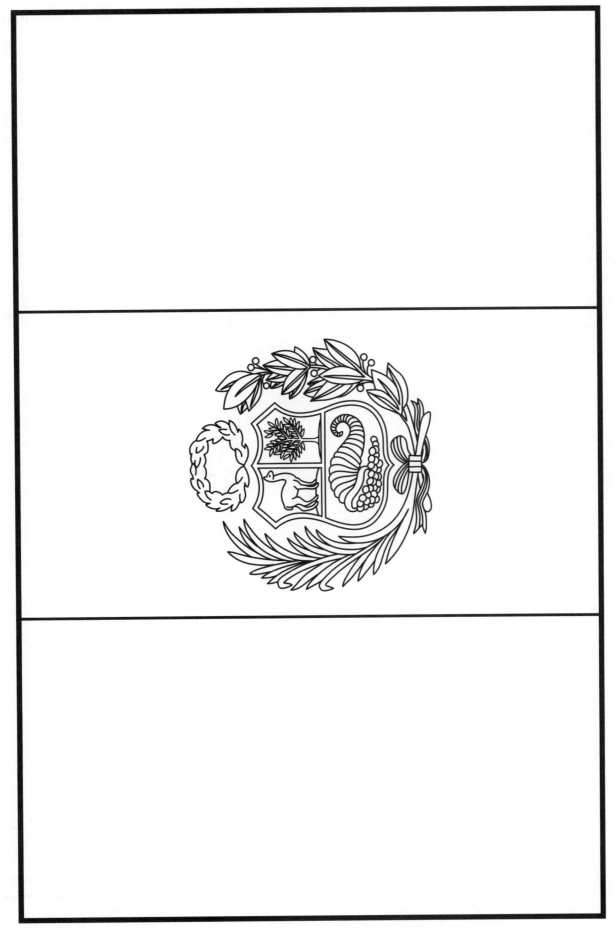

The Flag of Peru

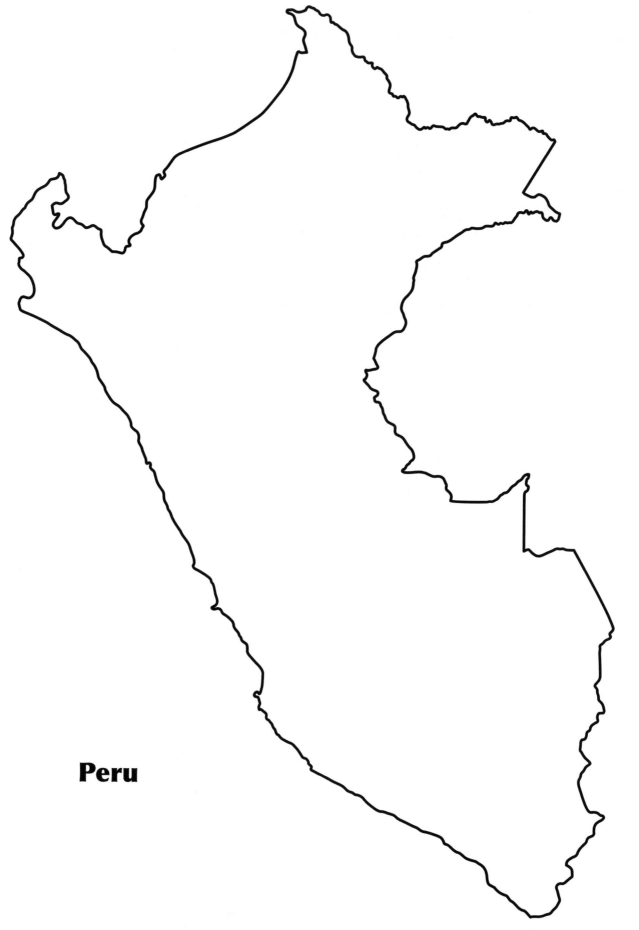

Peru

© Carson-Dellosa • CD-104263

Additional Resources

Books

Braman, Arlette. N. *Secrets of Ancient Culture: The Inca*. Jossey-Bass, 2003.

George, Charles and Linda. *The Inca*. Blackbirch Press, 2005.

Heisey, Janet. *Countries of the World: Peru*. Gareth Stevens Publishing, 2001.

Henty, George Alfred. *The Treasure of the Incas*. BiblioBazaar, 2007.

Lawrence, Michael. *The Poppykettle Papers*. Chrysalis Children's Books, 2001.

Lyle, Garry. *Peru*. Chelsea House, 1998.

Lamasson, Patrick. Ed. *Peru: Art from the Chavín to the Incas*. Skira, 2006.

Morrison, Marion. *Peru*. Children's Press, 2000.

Web Sites

CIA World Factbook—Peru.
https://www.cia.gov/library/publications/the-world-factbook/geos/pe.html

Go Places with Time for Kids—Peru.
http://www.timeforkids.com/TFK/specials/goplaces/0,12405,358684,00.html

Library of Congress Country Studies—Peru.
http://lcweb2.loc.gov/frd/cs/petoc.html

National Geographic—Peru.
http://www3.nationalgeographic.com/places/countries/country_peru.html

Welcome to Peru.
http://www.peru.info/perueng.asp

Onward to Chile

Area: 289,113 sq. miles (748,800 sq. km)
Capital City: Santiago
Population: 16,284,741
Main Language: Spanish
Main Religion: Roman Catholicism
Currency: Chilean peso
Government: Republic
Flag:

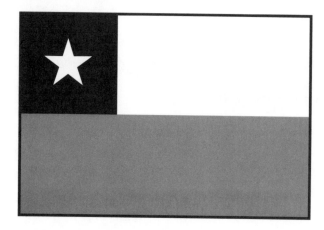

The flag of Chile, which was adopted in 1817, has two horizontal stripes. The top stripe is white and the bottom stripe is red. In the top left-hand corner over the white stripe is a blue square with a white star in the center. The red stripe represents the patriots who fought for independence, the white stripe symbolizes the snow of the Andes Mountains, and the blue represents the sky. The white star represents a guide to progress and honor.

For Your Information

Chile is located along the southwestern coast of South America and stretches over 2,700 miles (4,345 kilometers). Its width is never more than 150 miles (241 kilometers), which makes the country more than 18 times longer than it is wide. Chile borders the Pacific Ocean on the west. Chile's most noticeable geographical characteristic, apart from its narrowness, is the huge, almost impassable wall of the Andes Mountains. The Andes contain more than 50 volcanic peaks.

In the center of the country is a long, extensive river valley which is occupied in the north by large farms and in the south by forests and lakes. Santiago, the capital, is located in the more prosperous northern section of the central valley. The lake district in the south is home to Chile's native people, the Araucanians.

The Juan Fernández Islands and the famous Easter Island are two of Chile's possessions in the Pacific Ocean. Both of these are national parks. The Juan Fernández Islands are located approximately 416 miles (670 kilometers) off the Chilean coast, while Easter Island is located 2,297 miles (3,697 kilometers) away.

Only three percent of Chile has land that is suitable for farming; however, the country produces grapes, apples, pears, onions, wheat, corn, oats, beef, poultry, and timber. There has been a large increase in the export of fresh fruit and canned vegetables from Chile. In temperate central Chile, the primary crops are grains, potatoes, beans, rice, and a variety of vegetables. Industrial crops, such as sugar beets and sunflower seeds for cooking oil, are also common.

Chile, one of the foremost fishing nations in the world, produces sardines, jack mackerel, chub mackerel, hake, and anchovies. The principal products are fish meal and fish oil, which are shipped to Europe and the United States for the production of animal feed and industrial oil.

© Carson-Dellosa • CD-104263

Fascinating Facts

 Easter Island is a small, triangular-shaped island with an extinct volcano in each corner. It is famous for the hundreds of huge stone statues that were found when the island was discovered by Dutch explorers on Easter Sunday in 1722. The giant stone statues, called *Moai*, have caused people to wonder how they were carved and transported to their present locations. The average Moai statue weighs 80 to 90 tons (72–82 metric tons) and ranges from several feet to 30 feet in height.

 There are no major river systems in Chile; however, there are short rivers that begin in the Andes Mountains and flow west to the Pacific Ocean. Because of the rapids, these rivers are unnavigable, but they are used as an important energy source—hydroelectric power. Hydroelectric power stations produce about half of Chile's electricity.

 Santiago, the capital and largest city of Chile, has a population of more than 5 million people. Being one of the only cities in the world where people have easy access to both ski slopes and beaches makes Santiago a popular place to live. Lying on the Mapocho River, Santiago has a spectacular view of the Andes Mountains to the east. Santiago has been the capital of Chile since 1818.

 In 1704, Alexander Selkirk, a Scottish sailor, was abandoned by his captain on a deserted island in the Juan Fernández archipelago. Selkirk survived on the island for more than four years before he was rescued by a British ship. The novel *Robinson Crusoe* by Daniel Defoe was based on the story of Selkirk's adventure. In 1966, the government of Chile renamed the island "Isla Robinsón Crusoe."

 On September 18, 1810, Chile began its quest for independence from Spain. Today, this date is known as *Fiestas Patrias*, or Independence Day. This date is also the unofficial beginning of spring. (In the southern hemisphere, where Chile is located, the seasons are opposite of those in the northern hemisphere.) To celebrate Chile's independence, dance pavilions called *fondas* are set up in fields and in empty lots. Everyone dances the *cueca* and enjoys *empanadas* (pastries often filled with meat), a favorite national food.

 Chilean cowboys, called *huasos*, are part of Chile's national heritage. Each cowboy wears a traditional costume that includes a colorful poncho, a broad-brimmed felt or straw hat, and leather boots with huge spurs. These cowboys are well-known for their skills on horseback. The horses and cowboys work well together and can perform many impressive stunts.

 The first two days of November are part of the Day of the Dead celebration in Chile. This festival honors the dead and celebrates life. Originating in Mexico, this holiday combines rituals dedicated to the Aztec war god and rituals from the pagan holiday All Hallows Eve. Festivities include visiting family grave sites to decorate headstones and bring food offerings.

Spanish Language Activities

Slang Phrases from Chile

gallo	rooster; sometimes used to refer to a man
guagua	baby (from Quechua)
lolo/lola	teenager
mala pata	tough luck
los pacos	the police
pololo/polola	boyfriend/girlfriend
taco	traffic jam
USA (pronounced "yoosa" or "yuasay")	United States

Chilean Poem
by Pablo Neruda (1924)
Translated by W. S. Merwin

Es la mañana llena

Es la mañana llena de tempestad
en el corazón del verano.

Como pañuelos blancos de adiós viajan las nubes,
el viento las sacude con sus viajeras manos.

Innumerable corazón del viento
latiendo sobre nuestro silencio enamorado.

Zumbando entre los árboles, orquestal y divino,
como una lengua llena de guerras y de cantos.

Viento que lleva en rápido robo la hojarasca
y desvía las flechas latientes de los pájaros.

Viento que la derriba en ola sin espuma
y sustancia sin peso, y fuegos inclinados.

Se rompe y se sumerge su volumen de besos
combatido en la puerta del viento del verano.

The Morning Is Full

The morning is full of storm
in the heart of summer.

The clouds travel like white handkerchiefs of good-bye,
the wind, traveling, waving them in its hands.

The numberless heart of the wind beating
above our loving silence.

Orchestral and divine, resounding among the trees
like a language full of wars and songs.

Wind that bears off the dead leaves with a quick raid
and deflects the pulsing arrows of the birds.

Wind that topples her in a wave without spray
and substance without weight, and leaning fires.

Her mass of kisses breaks and sinks,
assailed in the door of the summer's wind.

Pablo Neruda was born in Chile in 1904. In 1971, he received the Nobel Prize for Literature. He was a well-known poet and diplomat.

© Carson-Dellosa • CD-104263

Recipes

Ensalada Chilena (Chilean Salad)

Ingredients:

2 medium onions, finely chopped
2 jalapeño chili peppers, seeded and finely chopped
6 large tomatoes, chopped
2 tsp. (10 mL) salt
2 tsp. (10 mL) pepper
6 tbsp. (89 mL) olive oil
3 tbsp. (44 mL) lemon juice
½ cup (118 mL) cilantro leaves, coarsely chopped

Directions:

Soak the chopped onions in cold water for approximately 10 minutes while preparing the other ingredients. Rinse and drain the onions in a colander. Combine the jalapeños, tomatoes, and onions in a large salad bowl. Season with salt and pepper. Drizzle with lemon juice and olive oil. Toss well. Sprinkle with cilantro. Yield: 8 servings

Porotos Granados (Beans with Vegetables)

Ingredients:

2 tbsp. (30 mL) vegetable oil
1 cup (237 mL) onion, finely chopped
3 cloves garlic, finely chopped
1 tsp. (5 mL) ground oregano
1 tbsp. (15 mL) paprika
1 cup (237 mL) zucchini, peeled and finely sliced
4 cups (946 mL) cooked, dried navy beans (save the liquid)
1½ cups (355 mL) water
1½ cups (355 mL) canned stewed tomatoes
1 cup (237 mL) corn kernels
salt
pepper

Directions:

Heat oil in large saucepan over medium-high heat. Add the onion, oregano, paprika, and garlic. Mix well. Sauté until the onion is soft (approximately three minutes). Add beans and zucchini and mix well. Add enough water to the saved bean liquid to equal two cups (474 mL) and add to mixture. Mix well and bring to a boil. Reduce heat and simmer. Add tomatoes, corn, and salt and pepper to taste. Simmer uncovered for approximately 30 minutes, making sure that the mixture does not dry out. Yield: 6 servings

Classroom Activities

Decoding Chile

Directions: Who is the famous Chilean man shown below? Answer each question using the Word Bank. Then, fill in the numbered blanks at the bottom of the page to decode the mystery.

1. ___ ___ ___ ___ ___ ___   ___ ___ ___ ___ ___ ___ is famous for its hundreds of stone statues.
            8   4

2. ___ ___ ___ ___ ___ ___ ___ ___ is the capital and largest city in Chile.
         2

3. ___ ___ ___ ___ ___ ___ ___ ___ *Crusoe* was based on the story about Alexander Selkirk.
            6

4. Chile's Independence Day is called ___ ___ ___ ___ ___ ___ ___ ___   ___ ___ ___ ___ ___ ___ ___.
                                        7   1

5. The ___ ___ ___   ___ ___   ___ ___ ___ ___ ___ celebration occurs in November.
        11   10

6. Chile produces sardines, jack mackerel, and ___ ___ ___ ___ mackerel.
                                                    3

7. The Chilean ___ ___ ___ ___ is the currency used in Chile.
                 5

8. ___ ___ ___ ___ ___ ___ are Chilean cowboys who are excellent horsemen.
     9

Word Bank

chub
Day of the Dead
Easter Island
Fiestas Patrias
huasos
peso
Robinson
Santiago

___ ___ ___ ___ ___
 1   2   3   4   5

___ ___ ___ ___ ___ ___
 6   7   8   9   10 11

© Carson-Dellosa • CD-104263

Classroom Activities

Making an *Arpillera*

For several decades, women in Chile have gathered to make *arpilleras*. These colorful pieces of art are created by urban women to show the way in which they live. Begun as a popular folk art, arpilleras show the true conditions of Chile.

Materials:
pieces of felt, 10" x 12" (25 cm x 30 cm), various colors
glue
scissors
grease pencils
library books and Web sites about Chile (see page 55)

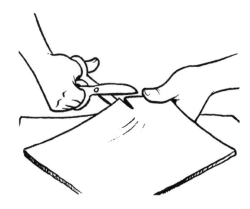

Directions:
1. Have each student research daily activities, scenes, famous places, and celebrations from Chile. Then, have him select a realistic scene or picture that he wishes to create.
2. Next, have each student use a grease pencil to draw the various people, places, or scenes for his arpillera.
3. Help each student cut the shapes from the felt.
4. Then, have each student select a sheet of felt to use for his background.
5. Tell each student to glue the shapes he has cut out in order by sticking the items that will appear farthest away to the background first.
6. Have each student continue gluing the shapes until he has completed his arpillera.
7. Ask each student to write a short paragraph describing his scene, famous place, or activity from Chile.
8. Display the arpilleras in the classroom or the media center.

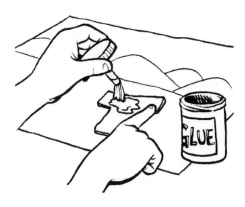

Classroom Activities

Creating a Moai

Help students create statues like the mysterious ones on Chile's Easter Island.

Step 1: Make Homemade Clay

Materials:
2¼–2½ cups (532–591 mL) flour
1 cup (237 mL) salt
1 tbsp. (15 mL) cooking oil
1¼ cup (296 mL) warm water
small plastic bags

Directions:
Mix 2¼ cup (532 mL) flour and the salt together in a bowl. Add the oil and stir. Then, slowly add the water and stir. Continue mixing until well blended. Knead the dough with your hands for approximately 10 minutes until it is smooth and firm. If the dough is too sticky, add the remaining ¼ cup (59 mL) of flour. If the dough is too dry, add a little more water. Place the dough in a resealable plastic bag to keep it from drying out and place in the refrigerator. The dough will last about one week.

Step 2: Create a Moai

Materials:
research materials about Easter Island (see page 55)
homemade clay or prepackaged self-hardening clay
plastic knife or plastic clay tools
wax paper
plastic coated paper plate

Directions:
1. As a class, research the Moai statues found on Easter Island.
2. Have each student place wax paper on her desktop or work space.
3. Instruct each student to use a ball of clay to shape a Moai statue.
4. Using the plastic knife or clay tools, each student should create the shape of the eyes, nose, mouth, and ears of the statue.
5. To air-dry the statues, place them on plastic coated paper plates and leave to dry for about five days (or until very hard). Have each student turn her statue over each day to be sure that all sides are drying.

   © Carson-Dellosa • CD-104263

© Carson-Dellosa · CD-104263

The Flag of Chile

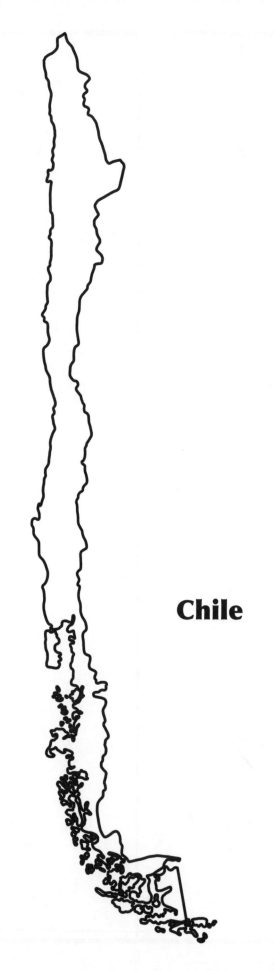

Chile

© Carson-Dellosa • CD-104263

Additional Resources

Books

Blomquist, Christopher. *A Primary Source Guide to Chile*. PowerKids Press, 2005.

Dipiazza, Francesca Davis. *Chile in Pictures*. Twenty-First Century Books, 2007.

Galvin, Irene Flum. *Chile: Journey to Freedom*. Dillon Press, 1996.

Hughes, Brenda. *Folk Tales from Chile*. Hippocrene Books, 1998.

Klingel, Cynthia and Robert B. Noyed. *Chile*. Compass Point Books, 2002.

Kwek, Karen, Melvin Neo, Jenette Donovan Guntly. *Welcome to Chile*. Gareth Stevens Publishing, 2004.

Martinez, Renee Russo and Leong Wen Shang. *Countries of the World: Chile*. Gareth Stevens Publishing, 2002.

Pickering, Marianne. *Chile: Where the Land Ends*. Benchmark Books, 1997.

Pitcher, Caroline. *Mariana and the Merchild: A Folk Tale from Chile*. William B. Eerdmans Publishing, 2000.

Weber, Valerie J. *I Come from Chile*. Weekly Reader, 2006.

Web Sites

CIA World Factbook—Chile.
https://www.cia.gov/library/publications/the-world-factbook/geos/ci.html

Library of Congress Country Studies—Chile.
http://lcweb2.loc.gov/frd/cs/cltoc.html

Lonely Planet—Chile.
www.lonelyplanet.com/worldguide/destinations/south-america/chile-and-easter-island/

National Geographic—Chile.
http://www3.nationalgeographic.com/places/countries/country_chile.html

U.S. Department of State—Chile.
http://www.state.gov/r/pa/ei/bgn/1981.htm

Traveling to Spain

Area: 192,874 sq. miles (499,542 sq. km)
Capital City: Madrid
Population: 40,448,191
Main Language: Castilian Spanish
Main Religion: Roman Catholicism
Currency: Euro
Government: Parliamentary monarchy
Flag:

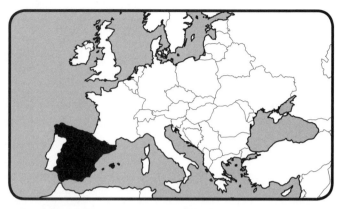

The current flag of Spain, adopted in 1981, contains three horizontal stripes. The two outer stripes are red. The middle stripe is yellow, and it is twice as tall as the red stripes. The Spanish coat of arms is on the hoist side (the side of the flag that is attached to a flagpole or staff) of the yellow band. The coat of arms has two crown-topped pillars with red banners showing the motto in Latin, *Plus Ultra*, which means "more beyond."

For Your Information

Located in southwestern Europe, Spain is Europe's fourth largest country following Russia, Ukraine, and France. The Spanish mainland occupies 85 percent of the Iberian Peninsula, which it shares with Portugal. Spain also controls the Balearic Islands in the Mediterranean Sea and the Canary Islands in the Atlantic Ocean off the coast of Morocco. A broad central plateau is located in the south and east of the country. It is crossed by a series of mountain ranges and river valleys. The main rivers in Spain are the Ebro in the northeast, the Tajo in the central region, and the Guadalquivir in the south.

After Switzerland, Spain is considered the most mountainous country in Europe, with an average height above sea level of 2,130 feet (650 meters). The Pyrenees Mountains are located along Spain's northern border. The Cantabrian Mountains are in the northwest. The Sierra de Guadarrama are found in central Spain, and the snowcapped peaks of the Sierra Navada and Sierra Morena are located in the south. Spain's tallest mountain, Pico de Teide, is located on the island of Tenerife. The highest mountain on the mainland is Pico de Mulhacén.

Spain's rugged landscape results in a range of temperatures and climates. In general, the climate is considered temperate with clear, hot summers in the interior of the country and more moderate and cloudy weather along the coasts. Winters in the interior are cloudy and cold, but along the coasts they are partly cloudy and cool.

The old Spanish currency, the peseta, was replaced by the European Union currency, the euro, in 2002. Spain's economy is now related to the economy of the European Union. The major agricultural products of Spain include grains, poultry, pork products, fresh fruits, olives, wine, and vegetables. The main exports include cars, chemicals, footwear, fruits, vegetables, fuel, and refined oil products.

Wildlife in Spain includes rabbits, partridges, lynx, wildcats, wolves, foxes, wild boars, mountain goats, and deer. Bird life includes the rare golden eagle. Fish, such as trout and barbell, can be found in Spain's mountain lakes and streams. Sea life, including tuna, sardines, and dolphins, can be found off the Atlantic coast, and octopuses and squid can be found off the Mediterranean coast.

© Carson-Dellosa • CD-104263

Fascinating Facts

A very important part of Spanish culture is the flamenco, a special kind of music and dance. The music is used as a way to express all kinds of feelings, such as sadness, happiness, love, and hatred. The rhythm and mood of flamenco is created using guitars and voices. The dancers use intricate hand movements.

Bullfighting, known as the *fiesta nacional* (national festival), is celebrated more in some parts of Spain than others. All of the men who fight bulls in a *corrida de toros* (bullfight) are *toreros* (bullfighters). The matador is the main torero. He is the one who kills the bull at the end of the fight. Some matadors are famous throughout Spain and even in Latin America. The best bullfighters are millionaires. Bullfighting is controversial in Spain today. Many Spaniards believe it should no longer be practiced. Others believe it is the symbol of Spain that makes it different from other countries.

The Alcázar, located at the intersection of the Clamores and Eresma Rivers in the city of Segovia, is part military fortress and part palace. It was built in the late 11th century by King Alfonso VI. The castle has many underground levels and secret passages leading to the rivers and nearby palaces.

Each region in Spain and each of the 8,000 small towns and villages has a special day it celebrates as its own. In the Spanish region of Catalonia in the town of Tarragona, human pyramid building is serious. It is practiced at town festivals. For hundreds of years, *castellers* (human pyramid builders) have used their bodies to form skyscrapers as tall as five-story buildings.

Pamplona, the capital city of the region of Navarra, is best known for the annual running of the bulls which draws tourists from all over the world. The city celebrates the feast of San Fermin (the town's patron saint) by releasing bulls to run through the streets to the bullring. Many people risk their lives to run with the bulls. The event is divided into two parts. First, the bulls run through the streets. Next, young bulls with padded horns are let loose in the crowd at the bullring.

Participants in *La Tomatina*, an annual fiesta in Buñol, Valencia, throw thousands of tomatoes at each other in a huge food fight. Large cartloads of ripe tomatoes are driven into the main square where thousands of people throw tons of tomatoes at each other. The festival is held on the last Wednesday of August.

The Alhambra palace in Granada is a superb example of Islamic architecture. The palace was built by Ibn al-Ahmar and his successors, who were Moorish kings of Granada. The Alhambra was originally built as a fortress containing a palace and a small city. The interior walls are intricately carved with scenes of men and nature.

Chupa Chups are a brand of gourmet lollipops created in Spain in the early 1950s. They are sold in 170 countries around the world. The Chupa Chups company sells four billion lollipops each year in 40 different flavors. In 1969, Spanish artist Salvador Dali designed the logo for these lollipops. Madonna, Elton John, Sheryl Crow, and Magic Johnson are among the many famous people who have promoted Chupa Chups.

Spanish Language Activities

Did you know that there are actually four different languages spoken in Spain? Castilian Spanish, Catalan, Basque, and Galician are the four main languages of Spain. Almost everyone in Spain knows how to speak Castilian Spanish; however, Catalan is the second main language with approximately 7 million speakers in the northeast region of Catalonia. Basque is spoken by approximately 520,000 people in the Spanish Basque Country provinces. In the northwest corner of Spain, especially in Galicia, an estimated 1.5 million people speak Galician.

Spanish Poem

by Federico García Lorca
Translated by John A. Crow

Mi niña se fue a la mar

Mi niña se fue a la mar,
a contar olas y chinas,
pero se encontró, de pronto,
con el río de Sevilla.

Entre adelfas y campanas
cinco barcos se mecían,
con los remos en el agua
y las velas en la brisa.

¿Quién mira dentro la torre
enjaezada, de Sevilla?
Cinco voces contestaban
redondas como sortijas.

El cielo monta gallardo
al río, de orilla a orilla,
en el aire sonrosado,
cinco anillos se mecían.

My Child Went to the Sea

My child went to the sea
To count the waves and shells,
But at Seville's wide river,
She stopped and looked for me.

Five spotless ships were rocking
Between the flowers and bells,
Their oars were in the water
Their keels riding in the swells.

Who sees inside the dazzling
Gold tower of Seville?
Five hidden voices answered,
Five rounded rings they fill.

The sky mounted the river
From shore to shining shore,
And in the russet twilight
Rocked five rings, not one more.

© Carson-Dellosa • CD-104263

Recipes

Paella (Chicken and Seafood Dish)

Ingredients:
½–1 lb. (0.227 kg–0.454 kg) shrimp, unpeeled
1 lb. (0.454 kg) scallops
3 skinless chicken breasts, cut into chunks
2 tbsp. (30 mL) chicken bullion
1 small onion, minced
2 green peppers, sliced
1 red pepper, sliced
1 cup (237 mL) tomato sauce
2–3 cloves garlic, crushed
3–5 tbsp. (45–74 mL) minced fresh parsley
½ tsp. (2.5 mL) saffron
⅓ cup (79 mL) olive oil
1 tsp. (5 mL) sugar
4 cups (946 mL) rice
7 cups (1.7 L) water
salt

Directions:
Sauté the onions, parsley, and garlic in olive oil in a skillet until the onions begin to appear clear. Add saffron, chicken bullion, chicken, peppers, and sauté until chicken becomes white. Add tomato sauce and sugar. Stir. Add rice and water and bring to a boil. Salt to taste. Boil for five minutes, stirring occasionally. Add shrimp and scallops; boil an additional five minutes, stirring occasionally. Simmer for 10 minutes covered, stirring occasionally. If the rice appears to be dry during the last 10 minutes, add more water. If the rice is too wet at the end of the 10 minutes, uncover and evaporate unwanted liquid. Yield: 6 servings

Flan (Custard)

Ingredients:
1½ cups (355 mL) sugar
6 eggs
1 qt. (0.95 L) whole milk
1½ tsp. (7 mL) vanilla extract

Directions:
Preheat oven to 325ºF (170ºC). Spread ¾ cups of sugar evenly in the bottom of a heavy saucepan and place over medium-low heat to caramelize. Without stirring, watch the sugar closely as it begins to melt at the edges. It should first turn into a yellow syrup, then a golden syrup, and finally into a brown caramel sauce. When the liquefied sugar is turning from golden to brown, immediately remove the pan from the heat. In a separate bowl, beat the eggs until they are lemon colored. Add ¾ cups (177 mL) of sugar, the milk, and the vanilla. Mix thoroughly. Pour the mixture into the pan on top of the caramelized sugar. Bake for one hour (or longer) until a knife inserted in the flan comes out clean. Yield: 6 servings

Classroom Activities

Creating a Carnival Mask

Carnival is celebrated two weeks before the Christian observance of Lent. It is celebrated in many countries around the world, including Spain. Celebrations involve large parades in which people dress in costumes and wear masks.

Materials: (per student)
1 medium balloon
1 rubber band
1 cup (237 mL) starch
newspaper cut into strips
glue
grease pencil
tempera paint (red, black, white, yellow)
paintbrushes
2" (5 cm) plastic foam ball, cut in half
scissors
stapler
yarn (black, brown, or yellow)
1 piece of scrap cloth, approximately
        1 sq. yd. (0.84 sq. m)
masking tape

Directions:
1. Help each student inflate a balloon and close the end with a rubber band.
2. Next, have each student coat her entire balloon with starch.
3. Have each student glue newspaper strips onto her balloon and let the glue dry.
4. After the glue dries, have each student remove the rubber band and pull the balloon out of its "covering."
5. Instruct each student to draw a face on her mask and paint it.
6. Have each student glue the halves of the plastic foam ball on the mask face and paint them so that they look like eyes.
7. Help each student trim the bottom of her mask so that it can be worn comfortably on the top of her head.
8. Have each student staple the cloth around the bottom of her mask to create a cloak.
9. If the student wishes to wear her mask, help her cut holes in the cloak to see through.
10. To create hair, have each student wind yarn around her hand to form a thick bundle. Have her tie the bundle at one end with a piece of yarn and cut the other end. Instruct her to tape the mop of hair to her mask head to create hair.

© Carson-Dellosa • CD-104263

Classroom Activities

Spain in a Bag

Use a lunch bag to create a unique report about Spain.

Materials:

library books and Web sites about Spain
    (see page 65)
travel magazines or brochures about Spain
paper lunch bags
colorful pencils or markers
scissors
construction paper
fabric scraps
glue or glue sticks
craft sticks
index cards

Directions:

1. Have students research information about Spain. Some suggested information may include: capital city, current leader, tourist attractions, famous landmarks, geography, history, map of the country, famous people, economy, flag, climate, and natural resources.
2. Have each student draw or glue pictures that relate to Spain on the front of his bag.
3. Then, on one side of the bag, have him create a time line of historical events in Spain.
4. On the other side of the bag, have him make a list of famous landmarks, famous people, or major landforms.
5. On the back of the bag, have each student draw and color the flag of Spain and a map of the country, showing major rivers, mountains, and cities.
6. Next, have each student create puppets of three or four famous people from Spain, using glue or a glue stick, fabric scraps, markers, construction paper, and craft sticks.
7. Ask each student to gather or create two or three small items that represent Spain, such as toys, coins, etc.
8. On the index cards, have each student list five questions about Spain that he has learned from his research.
9. Have each student present his "Spain in a Bag" to the class. Then, display each bag in the media center.

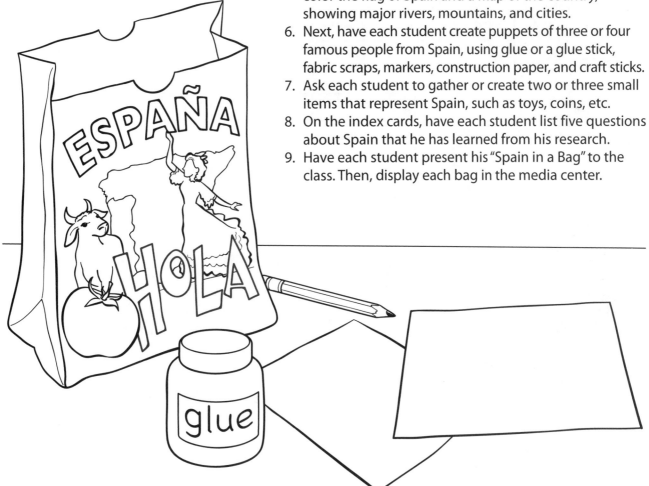

Crossword Puzzle

Directions: Complete the crossword puzzle using the clues.

Across:

1. the type of Spanish used as the main language in Spain
3. the peninsula Spain shares with Portugal
5. The tallest mountain on mainland Spain is Pico de _____.
6. the location of the running of the bulls
7. bullfighters in Spain
8. the currency now used in Spain
10. a castle in Segovia built in the 11th century
11. the annual fiesta where thousands of tomatoes are thrown
12. mountains that go across the north of Spain

Down:

2. an Islamic palace in Granada
4. a river located in the northeast of the country
5. the capital of Spain
6. the currency formerly used in Spain
9. islands in the Atlantic Ocean controlled by Spain

                                   © Carson-Dellosa • CD-104263

VLTRA

PLVS

The Flag of Spain

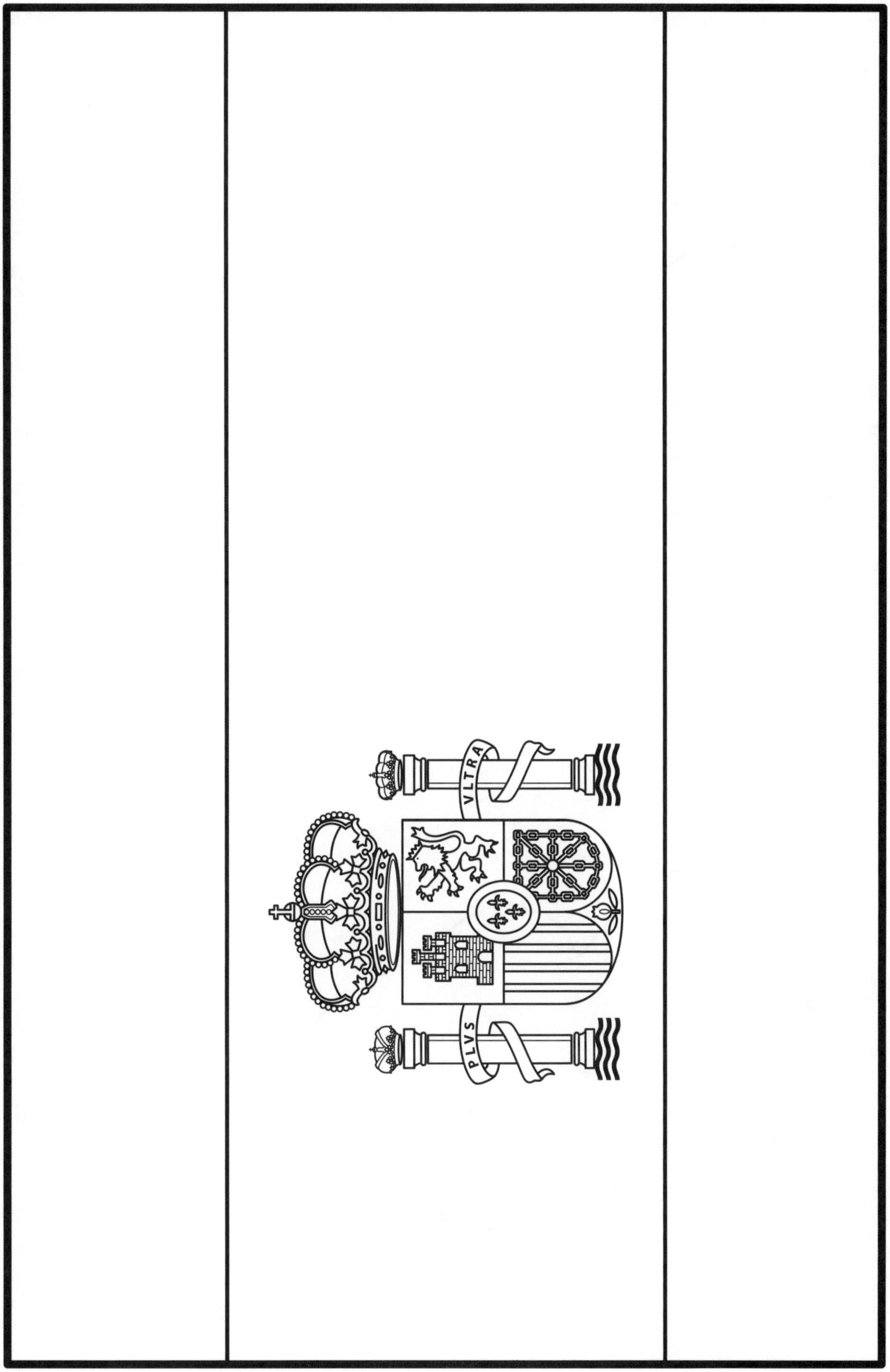

Spain

© Carson-Dellosa • CD-104263

Additional Resources

Books

Carr, Raymond, ed. *Spain—A History*. Oxford University Press, 2001.

Crow, John A. ed. *An Anthology of Spanish Poetry*. Louisiana State University Press, 1980.

Grinsted, Katherine. *Countries of the World: Spain*. Gareth Stevens Publishing, 2000.

Faiella, Graham. *Spain: A Primary Source Cultural Guide*. Rosen Publishing, 2004.

Lye, Keith. *Getting to Know Spain*. Passport Books, 1989.

Shubert, Adrian. *The Land and People of Spain*. Harper Collins Publishers, 1992.

Taus-Bolstad, Stacy. *Spain in Pictures*. Lerner Publishing, 2004.

Williams, Mark. *The Story of Spain*. Santana Books, 2000.

Web Sites

CIA World Factbook—Spain.
https://www.cia.gov/library/publications/the-world-factbook/geos/sp.htm

Fact Monster—Spain.
www.factmonster.com/ipka/A0107987.html

Library of Congress Country Studies—Spain.
http://lcweb2.loc.gov/frd/cs/estoc.html

Lonely Planet—Spain.
http://www.lonelyplanet.com/worldguide/destinations/europe/spain/

National Geographic—Spain.
http://www3.nationalgeographic.com/places/countries/country_spain.html

Approaching the United Kingdom

Area: 93,278 sq. miles (241,590 sq. km)
Capital City: London
Population: 60,776,238
Main Language: English
Main Religion: Christianity
Currency: British pound
Government: Constitutional monarchy
Flag:

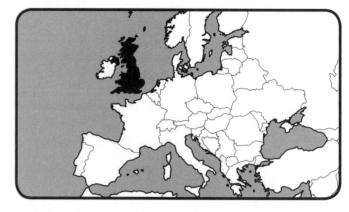

The flag of the United Kingdom is red, white, and blue and combines the crosses of St. George (the patron saint of England), St. Andrew (the patron saint of Scotland), and St. Patrick (the patron saint of Ireland). It is commonly called the "Union Jack," but the official name is the Union Flag.

For Your Information

The United Kingdom consists of the island of Great Britain—which includes England, Wales, and Scotland—and Northern Ireland. The name "Britain" is sometimes used to refer to the United Kingdom as a whole. England is approximately 50,000 square miles (129,500 square kilometers) and makes up just over half of the total area of the United Kingdom. To the west is Wales and to the north is Scotland. Northern Ireland is directly west of Great Britain across the Irish Sea. It makes up approximately 15 percent of the island that it shares with the Republic of Ireland. Great Britain is a land of wide geographical variety, especially in Wales and Scotland. The landscape includes mountains, lakes, and forests. The highest point in Great Britain is Ben Nevis, which is located in Scotland.

The United Kingdom has made important contributions to the world economy, especially in the areas of technology and industry. The United Kingdom's main exports since the end of World War II have been cultural, including literature, theater, film, television, and popular music. Perhaps the country's greatest export has been the English language, which is now spoken in almost every corner of the world. Scotland's main exports include personal computers, electronics, office equipment, semiconductors, and software. Although England and Ireland have few natural resources, England exports defense equipment, pharmaceuticals, oil and gas products, chemicals, and other manufactured goods. Agriculture, cattle ranching, and fishing are important to the economy of Ireland.

In Ireland, the general population is well-educated, with more than a 75 percent graduation rate from secondary schools. At 99 percent, England has one of the highest literacy rates in the world. At the ages of 7, 11, and 14, students in the United Kingdom are given a national test to help the schools decide what courses students should take. After the age of 16, many students go straight to the workforce or attend vocational schools. But, increasingly, more working class students are attending universities. In Scotland, students attend elementary school for seven years. After elementary school, students attend junior high school for four years and then take an examination. Those who pass go to senior high school for one or two years. After one year of senior high school, students take five examinations. Passing these examinations permits entrance to a university.

© Carson-Dellosa • CD-104263

Fascinating Facts

Early settlers in England created impressive arrangements of huge stones, but their purpose is still a mystery. Some of these stone creations, like Stonehenge (built sometime between 3,000 and 1,000 B.C.), are still standing today. In ancient times, there were no cranes or trucks to move these large stones. Therefore, large numbers of people must have worked for hundreds of years to create these stone structures. Some of the stones are from the Prescelly Mountains in Wales, which is 150 miles (241 kilometers) away from the site.

The monarch (king or queen) of the United Kingdom plays a mostly symbolic role in government as commander-in-chief of the armed forces and head of the Church of England and the Commonwealth. Even though the monarch is called the supreme head of the three branches of government, the "Crown" cannot make decisions without the advice of ministers and other leaders.

In 1999, Scotland's government had a major change, and a Scottish parliament was reestablished. Scotland can now act on many issues that directly affect its own people, such as housing, health, and economic development. Scotland is also represented by 72 ministers of parliament in the House of Commons in London.

Cricket, considered the most English of games, is played throughout the world, especially in former British colonies. The rules are complicated, but the object of the game is to score runs by hitting a hard, red ball with a straight bat made of wood. Two teams made of 11 players each play on a large grass field. In addition to cricket, other favorite sports include soccer (called *football* in the United Kingdom), rugby, and tennis.

In Ireland, the traditional Irish dance, or step dance, has increased in popularity as a result of a renewed interest in Irish culture. Sunday village dances have been the center of social life in rural areas since the 1600s. These dances, called *Ceilis* (pronounced "Kay-lees"), combine traditional dancing and music. Step dancing originated from the ceilis. Performed almost entirely with the legs and feet, step dancing has four groups of single dancers or four pairs of dancers standing in a square.

The most recognizable musical instruments in Scotland are the bagpipes. They are used frequently to accompany Highland dances. The pipes and drums led Scottish soldiers into battle for centuries and struck fear into the hearts of their enemies. There are two types of Scottish bagpipes: the Lowland bagpipe, which is blown by a bellows held under the piper's arm, and the Highland bagpipe, which is blown using the mouth.

Welsh cuisine shares many similarities with Western culture, including fast food restaurants and processed foods. Some traditional dishes remain popular, including *cawl* (a light soup containing lamb), Welsh cakes (small fruit scones cooked on a griddle), *bara brith* (a rich fruit bread), and laver bread (a red seaweed typically fried with oatmeal and clams).

© Carson-Dellosa • CD-104263

Language Activities

Common English Words in the United Kingdom

bangers	sausages	*fizzy drinks*	soft drinks
biscuit	cookie	*flat*	apartment
bobby	police officer	*lift*	elevator
brolly	umbrella	*petrol*	gasoline
car park	parking lot	*plimsolls**	sneakers (**daps* in Wales)
chips	french fries	*serviette*	napkin (usually paper)
cornet	ice cream cone	*telly*	television
Elastoplast®	adhesive bandage	*tube*	London subway system

The National Anthem of Wales*

(*Only first verse and chorus is shown.)

Hen Wlad Fy Nhadau

Mae hen wlad fy nhadau yn annwyl i mi,
Gwlad beirdd a chantorion, enwogion o fri;
Ei gwrol ryfelwyr, gwladgarwyr tra mâd,
Tros ryddid gollasant eu gwaed.

Gwald, gwald, pleidiol wyf i'm gwlad
Tra môr yn fur i'r bur hoffbau,
O bydded i'r heniaith barhau.

Land of My Fathers

The land of my fathers is dear unto me,
Old land where the minstrels are honored and free;
Its warring defenders, so gallant and brave,
For freedom their life's blood they gave.

Land, Land, true am I to my Land,
While seas secure this land so pure,
O may our old language endure.

The Flag of Wales

© Carson-Dellosa • CD-104263

Recipes

Shepherd's Pie (Meat & Vegetable Casserole)

Ingredients:
2 lb. (0.91 kg) ground beef
1 cup (237 mL) beef broth
4 cups (946 mL) cooked mashed potatoes
½ cup (118 mL) cheddar cheese, shredded
1 onion, chopped
2 carrots, peeled and sliced in thin rounds
½ cup (118 mL) chopped celery
2 tbsp. (30 mL) vegetable oil
2 tbsp. (30 mL) all-purpose flour
½ cup (118 mL) melted butter or margarine
salt
pepper

Directions:
1. Preheat oven to 350ºF (180ºC).
2. Heat oil in skillet over medium-high heat. Add celery, carrots, and onions and sauté for approximately three minutes, or until onions are tender. Add meat and reduce heat to medium. Stir continuously. Cook for approximately eight minutes or until meat is brown.
3. In a small bowl, add flour to the beef broth and mix. Then, add to the meat mixture and mix well. Season with salt and pepper and remove from heat. Transfer mixture to a baking pan.
4. Mix the mashed potatoes with ¼ cup (59 mL) melted butter, and salt and pepper to taste. Spoon the potatoes on top of the meat mixture and pour remaining butter over potatoes. Add cheese. Bake for 10 minutes or until the potatoes begin to brown and the cheese melts. Yield: 6–8 servings

Feather Fowlie (Scottish Chicken Soup)

Ingredients:
3 lb. (1.36 kg) chicken, cut into small pieces
6 cups (1.42 L) water
¼ cup (59 mL) parsley, finely chopped
3 tbsp. (45 mL) thyme
1 onion, finely chopped
2 celery stalks, finely chopped
3 egg yolks
¼ cup (59 mL) half-and-half
1 tsp. (5 mL) ground mace
salt
pepper

Directions:
1. In a saucepan, combine chicken, water, parsley, onion, celery, and thyme. Bring to a boil over high heat. Then, reduce heat and simmer for approximately 1½ hours until chicken is tender.
2. In a small bowl, combine egg yolks, half-and-half, and mace. Whisk until blended. Remove soup from heat. Add egg mixture to the soup, stirring constantly until well blended. Salt and pepper to taste. Yield: 6–8 servings

Classroom Activities

Making English Porcelain

English porcelain is famous around the world for its high standards of craftsmanship. It is still made in many traditional styles by skilled workers who paint intricate designs by hand.

Materials:
reference photos of English porcelain
paper plates
white copy paper or construction paper
pencils
rulers
colorful pencils or markers

Directions:
1. After looking at examples of English porcelain (right) as a class, have each student create a porcelain design using geometric shapes, flowers, birds, etc., on a piece of copy paper or construction paper.
2. Have each student sketch the design on her plate.
3. Using colorful pencils or markers, have each student complete her plate design.
4. Display the colorful plates on a bulletin board, in the media center, or in a hallway.

Recreating Stonehenge

Materials:
reference materials about Stonehenge
modeling clay or self-hardening clay
clay tools
cardboard or foam board
notebook and copy paper
pens or pencils

Directions:
1. Have students use the reference materials to research Stonehenge.
2. Have each student draw his version of Stonehenge on a sheet of copy paper.
3. Have each student follow his design to mold clay into a model of Stonehenge.
4. Have each student mount his model on cardboard or foam board.
5. Ask each student to write at least one paragraph explaining his theories about the origin and purpose of Stonehenge.
6. Display the models and have each student share his written work with the class.

 © Carson-Dellosa • CD-104263

Classroom Activities

Designing a Tartan

In Scotland, tartans have become a national symbol. A tartan is a plaid cloth design made up of stripes of varying width and color, usually patterned to identify a specific clan. The patterns were popular within certain areas of the country and were made of local wool. At one time, the only legal tartan was the Black Watch pattern, which was worn by the soldiers in Scotland.

Materials:
white construction paper
pencils
rulers
crayons, colorful pencils, or markers

Directions:
Show students several examples of tartan patterns, such as the Black Watch pattern (use the Internet, encyclopedias, or other sources). Have each student use a pencil and a ruler to measure and mark every inch at the top and bottom of the construction paper. Next, have each student connect these marks by drawing straight lines with a ruler. Then, each student should draw vertical lines in a pattern similar to the tartan shown below. Tell each student to choose two dark colors and one light color and color the stripes using the three colors. Display students' patterns in the classroom, in a hallway, or in the media center.

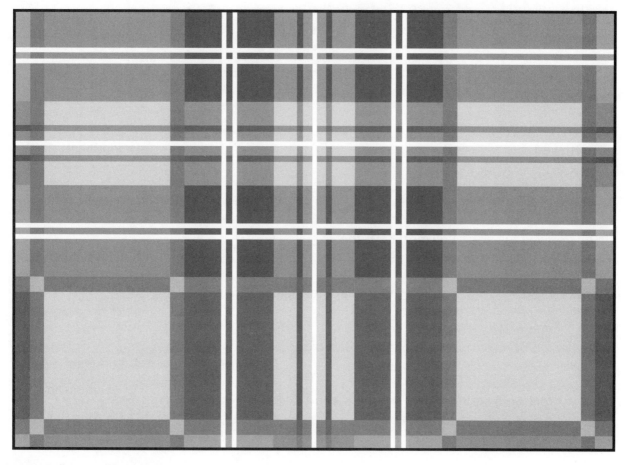

Map Activity

Directions: Use the map to answer the questions.

1. London is located in the _____ part of the United Kingdom.
   A. northwest   B. northeast   C. southeast   D. southwest

2. South of Edinburgh is the _____ River.
   A. Trent   B. Tweed   C. Thames   D. Carlisle

3. To go from Ayr to Belfast, you must cross the _____.
   A. North Atlantic Ocean   B. North Sea   C. North Channel   D. English Channel

4. Kirkwall is about _____ kilometers northeast of Thurso.
   A. 100   B. 150   C. 50   D. 25

5. All of the following are located along the coast of the North Sea except _____.
   A. Lewes   B. Scarborough   C. Aberdeen   D. St. Andrews

6. All of the following are located on the same island except _____.
   A. England   B. Scotland   C. Wales   D. Northern Ireland

                                                                    © Carson-Dellosa • CD-104263

The Flag of the United Kingdom

The United Kingdom

© Carson-Dellosa • CD-104263

Additional Resources

Books and Articles

Albyn, Carole Lisa and Lois Sinaiko Webb. *The Multicultural Cookbook for Students*. Oryx Press, 1993.

Britton, Tamara L. *Countries: Northern Ireland*. Checkerboard Books, 2003.

Gruffudd, Pyrs. "Wales." *Encyclopedia Britannica Deluxe Edition*. Encyclopedia Britannica, 2007.

Hull, Lise. *Scotland: Countries of the World*. Gareth Stevens Publishing, 2001.

Lister, Maree and Marti Sevier. *England: Countries of the World*. Gareth Stevens Publishing, 1998.

Sproule, Anna. *Great Britain: The Land and Its People*. Silver Burdett Press, 1991.

Web Sites

BBC News Country Profiles—the United Kingdom.
http://news.bbc.co.uk/1/hi/world/europe/country_profiles/1038758.stm

CIA World Factbook—the United Kingdom.
https://www.cia.gov/library/publications/the-world-factbook/geos/uk.html

National Geographic—the United Kingdom.
http://www3.nationalgeographic.com/places/countries/country_unitedkingdom.html

Oxfam Cool Planet—the United Kingdom.
http://www.oxfam.org.uk/coolplanet/ontheline/explore/journey/uk/ukindex.htm

U.S. Department of State—the United Kingdom.
http://www.state.gov/r/pa/ei/bgn/3846.htm

Touring Norway

Area: 118,704 sq. miles (307,442 sq. km)
Capital City: Oslo
Population: 4,627,926
Main Languages: Bokmal Norwegian and Nynorsk Norwegian
Main Religion: Christianity
Currency: Norwegian krone
Government: Constitutional monarchy
Flag:

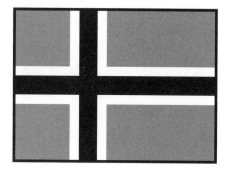

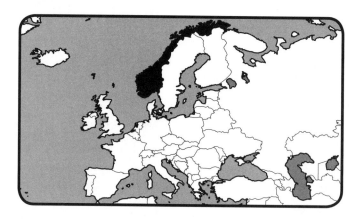

In 1821, the Norwegian parliament developed the flag design that is used today, although it faced a 77-year struggle to receive Swedish recognition. Designed by Frederik Meltzer, the Norwegian flag consists of a white cross on a red background (used in the Danish flag) with a blue cross on top for distinction.

For Your Information

Norway is a country in northern Europe that is located in the western half of the Scandinavian peninsula. Almost half of the country's inhabitants live in the far south around the capital city of Oslo. Approximately two-thirds of Norway is mountainous, with some 50,000 islands included as part of the country. The Barents Sea is located to the north, the Norwegian Sea and the North Sea are to the west, and the Skagerrak Strait is to the south. Norway borders land only on the east (with Sweden, Russia, and Finland).

Even though Norway is located at almost the same latitude as Alaska, its climate is warmer due to the Norwegian Current. This current carries 4–5 million tons (3.6–4.5 metric tons) of tropical water per second into the surrounding seas. The average yearly temperature on the west coast is 45°F (7°C). Western Norway has a marine climate with cool summers, moderate winters, and almost 90 inches (229 centimeters) of annual precipitation. Sheltered by the mountains, eastern Norway has an inland climate with warm summers, cold winters, and less than 30 inches (76 centimeters) of annual precipitation.

Norway has approximately 2,000 species of plants, including a wide variety of deciduous and evergreen trees. About half of Norway's total forest resources are located in the western part of the country. Reindeer, wolverines, lemmings, and other arctic animals are found throughout Norway. Elk can be found in the coniferous forests, and red deer are found on the west coast. A large variety of fish, especially trout and salmon, can be found in most of the rivers and lakes.

From ages 6 to 16, school attendance is mandatory for Norwegians. Required subjects in school include Norwegian, religion, mathematics, music, physical education, science, and English. In the upper grades, optional courses are available in the arts and other foreign languages, as well as vocational courses in areas like agriculture and seamanship. The country has four universities, all located in the capital city of Oslo. Only a few schools in Norway charge tuition, and all students are eligible for government loans.

© Carson-Dellosa • CD-104263

Fascinating Facts

 Reindeer are related to deer. They are called caribou in North America. Reindeer use their antlers to scrape away snow to graze on the moss and small plants beneath. The nomadic Samí people, or Lapps, drink reindeer milk and eat reindeer meat. Some Samí use reindeer hides to make their clothing and shelters.

 Northern Norway is often called the "Land of the Midnight Sun" because the land is lit by sunlight almost 24 hours a day for most of the months of May, June, and July. Unfortunately, during the months of December and January, it becomes the "Land of Noontime Darkness."

 The fjord horse, or *fjording,* is one animal for which Norway is well-known. This breed was probably domesticated more than 4,000 years ago. Fjord horses are good-natured and fairly small. The fjord horse was even shown on a Norwegian coin during the reign of King Olav V.

 The city of Oslo was founded by King Harold Hardrade around A.D. 1050, but the city did not become the capital until A.D. 1299. Oslo is located at the head of the Oslofjord. The city lies in a unique setting, with water along one side and mountains and hills on the other side.

 Alfred Nobel, a Swedish chemist and businessman, was the inventor of dynamite. He died a wealthy man, and in his will, he established a series of prizes for progress in science. These Nobel Prizes are awarded in Sweden. Nobel also left money to award a prize for achievements in working toward peace. He left decisions regarding the Nobel Peace Prize to the country of Norway, but no one knows why.

 Before 1850, snow skis were fastened to boots by leather straps around the toes. This method of attaching the skis restricted the movements that could be performed on skis. Then, a Norwegian man named Sondre Norheim made bindings out of branches that were soaked in water and allowed to harden into position. This improvement in skis allowed more foot movement, and skiing became an official sport. The first written manual on skiing, the first ski club, the first ski jump competition, and the first cross-country ski race all took place in Norway.

 Traditionally, several different instruments were used to play folk music in Norway. One of these instruments, the Hardanger fiddle, or *Hardingfele,* is now known as the official folk instrument of Norway. It has a shorter neck than a violin and eight strings instead of four. Four of the strings are played while the other four strings vibrate in response. This makes a droning sound that some have compared to the drone of a bagpipe.

 Because it is so available, many Norwegians eat seafood frequently. *Torsk,* or cod, is the basis for many meals. In every market in every coastal town, fish markets sell cod. *Lutefisk* is a dried codfish that has been soaked in lye, a very strong chemical. The lye changes the texture of the fish. Herring is also served in many different ways.

© Carson-Dellosa • CD-104263

Norwegian Language Activities

Common Words and Phrases		Numbers	
du	you	en	one
hva	what	to	two
nå	now	tre	three
God dag.	Good day.	fire	four
Morna.	Bye.	fem	five
mor	mother	seks	six
far	father	syv	seven
år	year	åtte	eight
Tusen takk.	Thank you very much.	ni	nine
		ti	ten

Norwegian Nursery Rhyme

(Ask students if "Little Trille" reminds them of a familiar nursery rhyme.)

Lille Trille

Lille Trille
satt på hylle.
Lille Trille
ramlet ned.
Ingen mann I dette land
Lille Trille bøte kan.

Little Trille

Little Trille
sat on a shelf.
Little Trille
Had a fall.
No man in this land
Could put Little Trille together again.

Norwegian Song

Ro, ro, ro din båt

Ro, ro, ro din båt,
Ta din åre fatt.
Vuggende, vuggende, vuggende, vuggende,
over Kattegatt.

Row, Row, Row Your Boat

Row, row, row your boat,
Gently down the stream.
Merrily, merrily, merrily, merrily,
Life is but a dream.

© Carson-Dellosa • CD-104263

Recipes

Lefse (Fried Potato Bread)

Ingredients:
4 cups (0.95 L) warm mashed potatoes
2 tbsp. (30 mL) milk
¼ cup (59 mL) vegetable oil
1 tsp. (5 mL) salt
2 cups (473 mL) all-purpose flour
butter
brown sugar or cinnamon

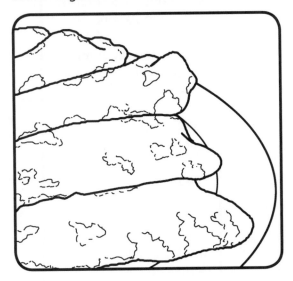

Directions:
1. Mix the mashed potatoes, vegetable oil, salt, and milk in a large bowl until smooth.
2. Cover and refrigerate mixture for two hours.
3. Place potato mixture onto a floured work surface and knead while adding the flour.
4. Divide the dough into 15 equal parts and roll each part into a ball.
5. Use a rolling pin to flatten each ball into an 8"–10" (20 cm–25 cm) circle. Add flour to prevent sticking.
6. Transfer to an ungreased skillet and cook over medium-high heat. Cook until blisters and brown spots appear (approximately one minute per side).
7. Repeat until all of the dough has been cooked. Stack the cooked circles between paper towels or wax paper.
8. Serve with butter or sprinkle with brown sugar or cinnamon. Roll or fold. Yield: 15 servings

Toskakake (Almond Caramel Topped Cake)

Ingredients:
3 eggs
1½ cups (355 mL) sugar
1½ cups (355 mL) all-purpose flour
1½ tsp. (7.5 mL) baking powder
1 cup (237 mL) melted butter
3 tbsp. (44 mL) milk
1 tsp. (5 mL) vanilla
½ cup (118 mL) heavy cream
½ cup (118 mL) chopped almonds

Directions:
Preheat oven to 350ºF (180ºC). In a large bowl, mix the eggs and 1 cup of sugar with a mixer for approximately five minutes until mixture is pale yellow. Set aside. In a separate bowl, combine the flour and baking powder. Add to the egg mixture using a whisk. Add ⅔ cup (158 mL) melted butter, milk, and vanilla. Mix. Pour into a greased cake pan. Bake for approximately 25 minutes. After the cake has been in the oven for 10–12 minutes, begin preparing the topping. Pour the remaining ⅓ cup (79 mL) melted butter in a skillet and cook over low heat. Add the remaining ½ cup (118 mL) of sugar and the cream. Stir continuously. Increase the heat to medium-high and bring to a boil. Boil for two minutes and then remove from heat. When the cake is done, remove from the oven and immediately pour the hot topping over the cake. Sprinkle with almonds and return to the oven. Continue baking for approximately 10 minutes until the top is bubbly and golden brown. Yield: 10–12 servings

Historical Time Line

Directions: Use the time line to answer the questions.

1. The Black Death occurred _____ years before Norway joined NATO.
   A. 200   B. 400   C. 600   D. 700

2. Olaf II Haraldsson became the first effective king of all of Norway in _____.
   A. 1349   B. 1015   C. 1039   D. 1814

3. Norway entered a political union with _____ before entering a union with Sweden.
   A. Denmark   B. Sweden   C. Germany   D. England

4. Prince Carl became king of Norway _____.
   A.   after German forces invaded the country
   B.   before the Black Death claimed many lives
   C.   after Norway entered a union with Sweden
   D.   after Norway became the world's second-largest exporter of oil

5. The German invasion of Norway occurred _____ years after Prince Carl became king.
   A. 45   B. 55   C. 135   D. 35

6. In _____, Norway joined NATO.
   A. 1905   B. 1940   C. 1949   D. 1995

7. Norway became the world's _____-largest exporter of oil in 1995.
   A. fifth   B. fourth   C. third   D. second

8. Germany controlled Norway for _____ years.
   A. six   B. four   C. five   D. seven

9. This time line covers _____ years in the history of Norway.
   A. 980   B. 880   C. 1080   D. 990

10. Norway entered a union with Sweden _____.
    A.   after Prince Carl became king
    B.   before Haraldsson became the first effective king
    C.   after German forces left Norway
    D.   before Norway joined NATO

1015—Olaf II Haraldsson became the first effective king of all of Norway.

1349—The Black Death wiped out 40–50 percent of the population.

1380—Norway entered into a political union with Denmark.

1814—Norway entered a union with Sweden.

1905—Prince Carl became King of Norway.

1940—Norway was invaded and overtaken by German forces.

1945—German forces left Norway and gave up control of the country.

1949—Norway joined the North Atlantic Treaty Organization (NATO).

1995—Norway became the world's second-largest oil exporter.

© Carson-Dellosa • CD-104263

The Flag of Norway

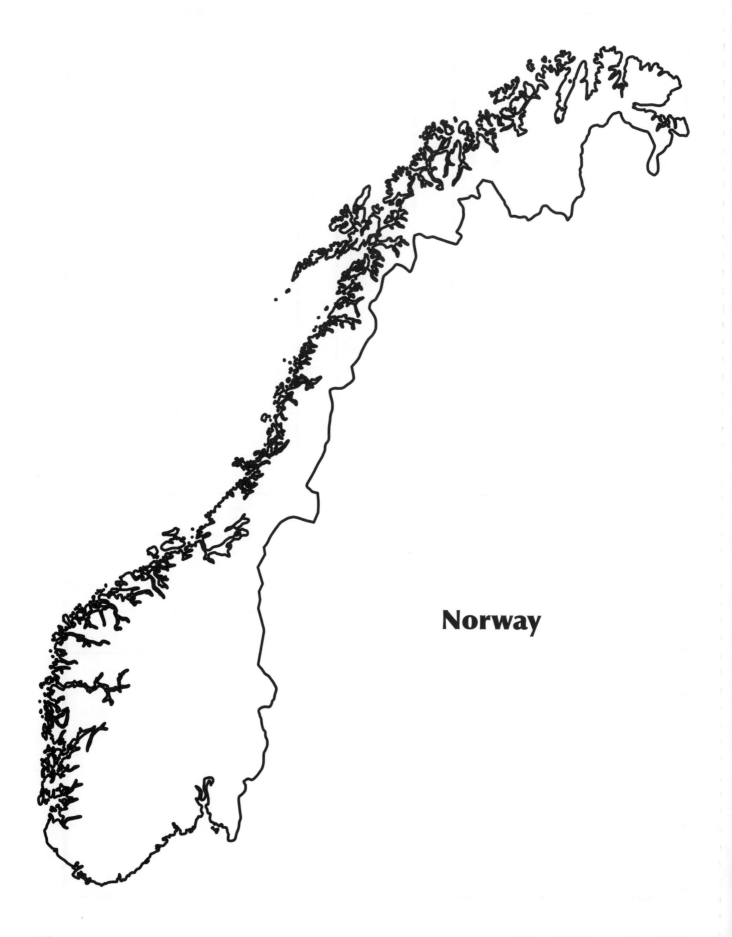

Norway

© Carson-Dellosa • CD-104263

Additional Resources

Books

Braun, Eric. *Norway in Pictures*. Lerner Publishing, 2002.

Blashfield, Jean F. *Norway: Enchantment of the World*. Children's Press, 2000.

Charbonneau, Claudette. *The Land and People of Norway*. Harper Collins Publishers, 1992.

Garrett, Dan. *World in View: Scandinavia*. Steck-Vaughn, 1991.

Kopka, Deborah L. *Ticket to Norway*. Carolrhoda Books, 2000.

Landau, Elaine. *Norway*. Children's Press, 2000.

McSwigan, Marie. *Snow Treasure*. Puffin Publishing, 2006.

Web Sites

BBC Country Profiles—Norway.
http://news.bbc.co.uk/1/hi/world/europe/country_profiles/1023276.stm

CIA World Factbook—Norway.
https://www.cia.gov/library/publications/the-world-factbook/geos/no.html

Lonely Planet—Norway.
www.lonelyplanet.com/worldguide/destinations/europe/norway/

National Geographic—Norway.
http://www3.nationalgeographic.com/places/countries/country_norway.html

Official Travel Guide to Norway.
www.visitnorway.com/

Landing in Iraq

Area: 166,859 sq. miles (432,162 sq. km)
Capital City: Baghdad
Population: 27,499,638
Main Languages: Arabic, Kurdish, Assyrian, and Armenian
Main Religion: Islam
Currency: New Iraqi dinar
Government: Parliamentary democracy
Flag:

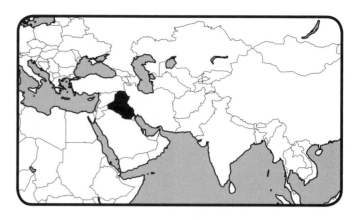

The Iraqi flag was adopted in 1963 and was modified slightly in 1991. The flag of Iraq has three equal horizontal stripes. The top stripe is red, the middle stripe is white, and the bottom stripe is black. The phrase "God is great" is written in Arabic in green on the white stripe. Three green stars are interspersed with the writing on the white stripe.

For Your Information

Cliffs are a distinct geographic feature of Iraq. The country is a little larger than the South American country of Paraguay. Iraq has four main geographic divisions: desert in the west and southwest, highlands in the north and northeast, dry grasslands between the Tigris and Euphrates rivers, and a plain through which the lower Tigris and Euphrates flow. The Tigris and Euphrates both begin in the highlands of Turkey. They join to form the Shatt al-Arab, which empties into the Persian Gulf. The highest point in Iraq is the peak of Haji Ibrahim at 11,812 feet (3,600 meters). The mountainous region of Iraq begins near the city of Mosul and stretches to the north and east.

Summer in Iraq lasts from May until October and has average temperatures of 70°F–110°F (20°C–43°C). Winter lasts from December until March, with an average temperature of 50°F (10°C). The country receives an average of only 4–7 inches (10–18 centimeters) of rain per year.

Iraq's largest export is oil. Other natural resources found in Iraq include natural gas, salt, sulfur, gypsum, and phosphates. Other major industries are food processing, textiles, and leather goods. Some important cash crops include wheat, dates, cotton, and barley. In the areas of Iraq that receive the most rain, the winter crop, which is mainly grain, is planted in the fall and harvested in the spring. Summer crops are grown in the areas in central and southern Iraq that need irrigation.

Many animals can be found in Iraq. The camel, mountain goat, deer, wild pig, fox, and wildcat are examples of mammals found there. A rodent called the jerboa is a tiny, mouse-like animal that lives in the desert region. Reptiles found in Iraq include snakes, lizards, and tortoises. There are also many bird species, including vultures, partridges, and hawks.

Family life is important in Iraq. Families are close and free time is often spent at home. Families are usually large, and extended family members often live in the same house. If a family grows larger, they add an extension onto their house called a *mushtamal*.

© Carson-Dellosa • CD-104263

Fascinating Facts

In the area that was once known as Mesopotamia that is now the country of Iraq, temples were originally built on platforms. Later, these were made higher and bigger, and eventually temples were built on stepped platforms. They were known as ziggurats. One of the most impressive ziggurats can be found at Aqarquf, a city west of Baghdad.

The *Ma'dan*, or Marsh Arabs, live in the marshy area of Iraq where the Euphrates and Tigris rivers meet. The Ma'dan live in triangular-shaped houses made of reeds that have no electricity, running water, or heat. These houses must be elevated to stay dry. By fishing and hunting, the Ma'dan live off the land. Each Ma'dan village has a guest house called a *mudhif* that is decorated with carpets and pillows.

Chanting, hand clapping, and drumming accompany traditional Iraqi music. One popular musical instrument is the *oud*. It is shaped like a gourd. A one-stringed, fiddle-like instrument called a *rebaba* is played by the Bedouin (nomadic Arabs). Finally, a tambourine called a *rigg* keeps the beat and adds accents to the music.

Southwest of the Euphrates River is a large desert region that extends into the countries of Jordan, Syria, and Saudi Arabia. Very few people live in this stony plain. It is lined with *wadis* (streams that are dry for most of the year but turn into rivers after a rain). During the winter season, rain sends dangerous flash floods down these wadis.

The Iraqis enjoy horse racing, soccer, chess, and backgammon. Basketball, volleyball, weight lifting, and boxing are also popular pastimes. Women in Iraq compete in such sports as volleyball, gymnastics, badminton, and swimming. They regularly compete in international competitions, such as the Muslim Women's Games. Leisure activities are usually centered around family events.

The Iraqi diet consists of flat bread, dates, rice, vegetables, and meat (chicken, fish, and grilled lamb). They also consume large amounts of fresh fruit, beans, and plain yogurt. *Sanbusak* (moon-shaped dough filled with cheese or meat) is a traditional dish eaten by the people of Iraq. Popular beverages in Iraq include tea, coffee, and fruit juice.

For some time, Iraq's Arabic culture has celebrated fine poetry. Poetry festivals attract many people in Iraq. Writers of both prose and poetry are honored. Iraqi poets, including a woman named Nazik al-Malaikah, are among the pioneers of free verse in Arabic. Theater and films are supported by the government. The 1,000-seat National Theater in Baghdad was one of the most modern in the Arab world when it was built. It has a revolving stage and two halls for movie projection.

© Carson-Dellosa • CD-104263

Arabic Language Activities

Counting

sifr	0	sitta	6
wahid	1	sab'a	7
ithnan	2	thmania	8
tholatha	3	tis'a	9
arba'a	4	ashra	10
khamsa	5		

Cultural and Geographical Words and Phrases

Dijlah	Tigris River
Al-Furat	Euphrates River
Hajj	pilgrimage to Mecca
Hejira	pilgrimage made by the Muslim prophet Muhammad
Shamal Garbi	northwesterly summer wind
Ganaob Sharqi	strong southeasterly winter wind
Shari'a	Islamic code of law
Wilayat	provinces of the Ottoman Empire

Arabic Alphabet

alif	ا	dal	د	daad	ض	khaf	ك
ba	ب	zal	ذ	tah	ط	lam	ل
ta	ت	ra	ر	zah	ظ	mim	م
tha	ث	zay	ز	eyn	ع	noon	ن
jem	ج	sín	س	ghyn	غ	ha	ه
ha	ح	shin	ش	pha	ف	waw	و
kha	خ	saad	ص	qaf	ق	ya	ي

© Carson-Dellosa • CD-104263

Recipes

Hadgi Badah (Cardamom Cookies)

Ingredients:
2 cups (473 mL) all-purpose flour
¼ tsp. (1.25 mL) baking powder
1 tsp. (5 mL) ground cardamom
½ tsp. (2.5 mL) salt
4 eggs
2 cups (473 mL) almonds, ground and blanched
1⅓ cups (315 mL) sugar
6 dozen almonds, whole

Directions:
1. Preheat oven to 350ºF (180ºC).
2. Sift the flour, baking powder, cardamom, and salt together.
3. In a separate bowl, beat the eggs and sugar until they are light and creamy.
4. Stir in the flour mixture and then add the ground almonds.
5. Drop dough by rounded tablespoons onto a greased baking sheet.
6. Slightly flatten the balls and place a whole almond in the center of each cookie. Bake for approximately 12 minutes.
7. Cool on a rack and store in an air-tight container. Yield: 48 cookies

Potato and Beef Kebba

Ingredients:
½ cup (118 mL) almonds, minced
¼ cup (59 mL) parsley, minced
1 lb. (0.45 kg) ground beef
1 lb. (0.45 kg) potatoes, boiled
2 eggs
¼ tsp. (1.25 mL) salt
¼ tsp. (1.25 mL) pepper
1½ cups (355 mL) bread crumbs

Directions:
1. Cook almonds, parsley, and meat in a saucepan on low heat for approximately 20 minutes.
2. Mash the potatoes.
3. Add the eggs and mix well.
4. Add the salt and pepper.
5. Shape the potato mixture into small rounded balls. Use a small amount of bread crumbs to keep the potato mixture from sticking to your hands.
6. Slightly flatten the mixture into patties no larger than your palm. Place meat in the center of each patty and fold one half over like a taco. Pinch the edges together to seal the meat inside.
7. Cover each patty with bread crumbs and reshape into a rounded, flat shape for frying.
8. Fry patties in hot oil on both sides until golden brown.
9. Serve hot with thousand island dressing, Vidalia onion dressing, or other sauce of your choice.
   Yield: 4–6 servings

Classroom Activities

Iraqi Clothing and Culture Collages

By studying the traditional clothing of the Iraqi people, students can learn about their culture.

Materials:
library books or Web sites about Iraqi culture, specifically
    clothing and leisure activities (see page 93)
colorful pencils or markers
poster board
glue or glue sticks
scissors
pieces of felt
scraps of cloth
yarn
construction paper
index cards

Directions:
1. As a class, use reference books, magazines, or Web sites to research traditional Iraqi clothing and common leisure activities.
2. Have each student sketch a scene of Iraqi life on a piece of poster board. Have him include both men and women in his scene.
3. Have each student use felt, cloth, or construction paper to create traditional Iraqi clothing for the people in his scene.
4. If desired, students can use yarn to give the people hair.
5. Instruct students to use colorful pencils or markers to draw facial features on the people.
6. Have each student write a paragraph on an index card describing the clothing worn by the women in his scene, along with the activities they are participating in.
7. On a second index card, have each student write a paragraph describing the clothing worn by the men in his scene, along with the activities they are participating in.
8. Display the collages on a bulletin board or in the media center.

© Carson-Dellosa • CD-104263

Classroom Activities

Arabic Numbers Memory Game

Copy and cut out the Arabic number word cards and the numeral cards. Play a memory matching game with students to help them learn Arabic numbers.

wahid	ithnan	tholatha	arba'a
khamsa	sitta	sab'a	thmania
tis'a	ashra	1	2
3	4	5	6
7	8	9	10

© Carson-Dellosa • CD-104263

Word Search

Directions: Find the words from the Word Bank in the word search. Words can go across, down, or diagonally.

Word Bank			
Arabic	Euphrates	oil	Tigris
Baghdad	Islam	oud	wheat
camel	Mesopotamia	ribaba	ziggurat
dates	mushtamal	rigg	

```
W B V T R M K V F O R N L M Q U D W R Y
L W G N L W Z A R I Q W L U V M R M I Y
Z Y I E J C H U R L N W N S X L P A B S
K A M C P R O E R A N C A H I Q S P A N
J A S B E U R Y A O B X Z T K H P N B A
C S P T X O S D S T F I O A L P O S A P
M D O L D U W A M I T Y C M S G H U I P
B A G H D A D T F I T C L A W X O N K I
O X K D F E X E S M S S E L J T J S T R
A F D E Z I V S W P S L F J A G I B M Q
C T G J J X D U E B R E U R D S Q V P J
A R L J T W P O S U M I U F I I S L A M
O J K A K M P H K D P G G R J K T D Z B
T S V V V J M J X R G H G G I U X C B C
O U D I U D B V Q I V I R L N F G Y S O
N K V B V G K P Z Y T G R A Y R W J O C
H Q M G D J P X H T B Z Z Y T X P C C D
A T S W F C C U L L C X D L E E J B J Q
U P N E R P Q P D C S Y V N O N S B A Q
M E S O P O T A M I A Z C O S T T A J B
```

© Carson-Dellosa • CD-104263

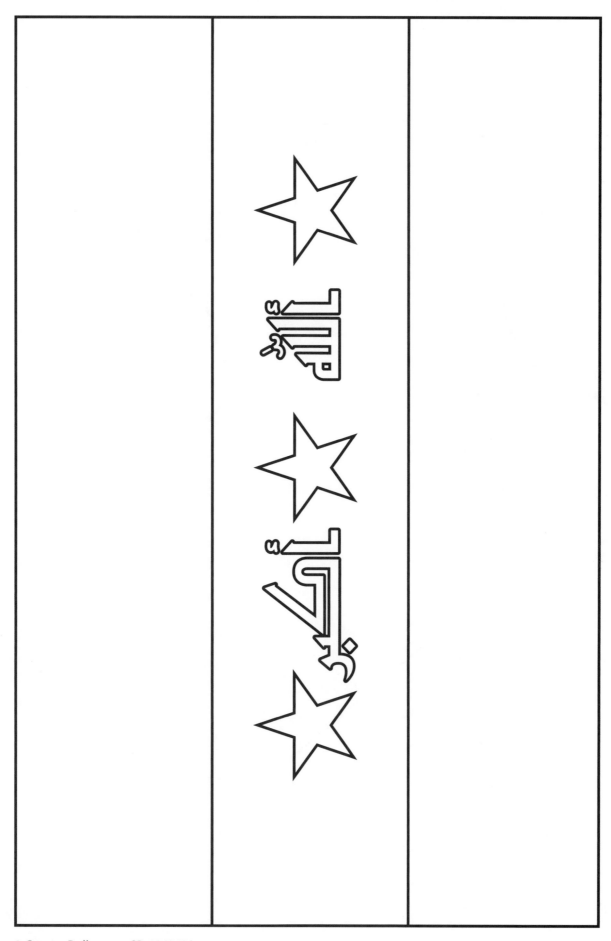

The Flag of Iraq

© Carson-Dellosa • CD-104263

Iraq

© Carson-Dellosa • CD-104263

Additional Resources

Books

Balcavage, Dynise. *Countries of the World: Iraq*. Gareth Stevens Publishing, 2003.

Docherty, John P. *Major World Nations: Iraq*. Chelsea House, 1998.

Dudley, William, ed. *Iraq: Opposing Viewpoints*. Greenhaven Press, 2003.

Foster, Leila Merrell. *Iraq: Enchantment of the World*. Children's Press, 1998.

Kotapish, Dawn. *Cities Through Time: Daily Life in Ancient and Modern Baghdad*. Runestone Press, 2000.

Spencer, William. *Iraq: Old Land, New Nation in Conflict*. Millbrook Press, 2000.

Web Sites

CIA World Factbook—Iraq.
https://www.cia.gov/library/publications/the-world-factbook/geos/iz.html

Library of Congress Country Studies—Iraq.
http://lcweb2.loc.gov/frd/cs/iqtoc.html

Lonely Planet—Iraq.
http://www.lonelyplanet.com/worldguide/destinations/middle-east/iraq/

National Geographic—Iraq.
http://www3.nationalgeographic.com/places/countries/country_iraq.html

U.S. Department of State—Iraq.
http://www.state.gov/p/nea/ci/c3212.htm

Voyage to Afghanistan

Area: 250,000 sq. miles (647,500 sq. km)
Capital City: Kabul
Population: 31,889,923
Main Languages: Afghan Persian (Dari) and Pashto
Main Religion: Islam
Currency: Afghani
Government: Islamic republic
Flag:

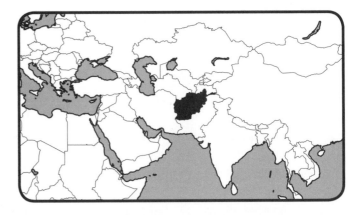

The flag of Afghanistan was adopted in 2002. It has three vertical stripes of black, red, and green. In the center of the red stripe is an emblem featuring a mosque with an arch (*mehrab*) and a many-tiered pulpit (*menber*).

For Your Information

Afghanistan is a landlocked country, which means that it is surrounded by land on all sides and has no coastline. To the north are the countries of Uzbekistan and Tajikistan. China borders the country to the northeast, Pakistan borders it to the east and south, and Iran and Turkmenistan border the country to the west and northwest. Afghanistan's shape is similar to a leaf, with the area of Wakhan in the northeast forming the stem.

Much of Afghanistan is covered with high mountains. The country's highest point, Nowshak Peak, reaches a height of 24,558 feet (7,485 meters) and is located in the northeastern part of the Hindu Kush Range along the border with Pakistan. The longest river, located entirely within the borders of Afghanistan, is the Helmand River, which is 715 miles (1,150 kilometers) long.

The climate of Afghanistan is characterized by hot summers and harsh winters. The mountainous regions in the northeast have a subarctic climate, but the mountainous areas that border Pakistan in the south have a wet, humid climate. Annual rainfall in Afghanistan varies from less than 3 inches (8 centimeters) in the west to 53 inches (135 centimeters) in the northeast.

Plant and animal life, which were once abundant in Afghanistan, have been greatly reduced due to war and environmental problems. In the nation's high mountains, pine and fir trees can be found. At the lower elevations, juniper, walnut, oak, alder, and ash trees grow. In the southern part of the country, there is very little vegetation because the land is covered with sandy deserts and dry regions. Jackals, wolves, foxes, and striped hyenas live in the mountains and foothills. A number of endangered species, including snow leopards, can also be found in these mountainous areas. Sheep, goats, and ibexes live in the Pamirs and the Hindu Kush Mountains.

Even though only six percent of the country's land area is under cultivation, agriculture dominates the economy of Afghanistan. The chief crop of the country is wheat. Other grains produced include barley, corn, and rice. Some of the most important exports are fruits, such as grapes, apricots, and figs.

© Carson-Dellosa • CD-104263

Fascinating Facts

Many people consider Afghanistan's mosques to be the nation's greatest works of art. One of these is the Blue Mosque, located in the city of Mazar-e Sharif. The city's name means "tomb of the saint." It is famous for a blue and gold tiled mosque and shrine that marks the location of a tomb. It is believed that the cousin and son-in-law of the prophet Muhammad is buried there. Afghans from around the country come to the city for the celebration of *Nawruz*. They come to see the raising of a green and pink flag which signals the start of spring and the beginning of the new year.

The men of Afghanistan cover their heads with a variety of head wear, including turbans and round caps. Most of the men wear turbans that are wrapped around a type of skullcap. Pashtun men tie their turbans so that one end of the cloth hangs down. However, in most other parts of the country, the men tuck in the ends of their turbans. While working in the fields, men wear only their skullcaps, not their turbans.

Women in Afghanistan wear either long, loose shirts over baggy pants or dresses. Unlike the men, most of the women in Afghanistan wear bright, colorful clothing. Because of the Islamic ideals of modesty, many women wear cotton or silk head scarves. Often, women adorn themselves with heavy jewelry, such as hair ornaments made of gold, silver, or lapis lazuli. Turquoise rocks are often used in Afghan jewelry because they are believed to keep away evil spirits.

Afghans are talented storytellers. Children spend many hours listening to family members tell detailed, creative stories. Stories for young children include rhymes with repeated words and sounds. Older children listen to stories with morals that teach them how to be good Muslims.

The country's national sport, *Buzkashi*, has been played for centuries and means "goat pulling." In this game, riders on horseback try to gain control of an animal carcass and carry it to the designated scoring area. The most skilled players, known as *chapandaz*, are often over the age of 40. Competition is quite fierce, and the winners receive prizes ranging from cash to fancy clothing. This game teaches teamwork and communication and is often played on special occasions, such as the new year and at weddings.

Kite flying, known as *gudiparan bazi*, is a popular sport in Afghanistan. Kites are made from tissue paper and bamboo frames. They come in a variety of sizes, ranging from 10 inches (25.4 centimeters) to five feet (1.5 meters) wide. Skilled kite flyers are good at understanding wind patterns. They are able to maneuver the kites and make them swoop dramatically. Large, flat fields throughout the country make excellent areas for flying kites.

Language Activities

Counting to Ten in Pashto

yaw	one
dwa	two
dray	three
saloar	four
pinza	five
shpag	six
woo'a	seven
atah	eight
naha	nine
las	ten

Days of the Week in Pashto

Yak Shanba	Sunday
Do Shanba	Monday
Say Shanba	Tuesday
Chaar Shanba	Wednesday
Panj Shanba	Thursday
Jumma	Friday
Shanba	Saturday

Everyday Pashto Expressions

Pashto	**English**
Za na poheegam.	I don't understand.
Za na yam khabar.	I don't know.
Sta nom (t)sa day(masc)/*da*(fem)?	What is your name?
Da (t)sa da(y)?	What is this?
Sta(so) Englisi zaba zda da?	Do you speak English?
Tashnab chari day?	Where is the bathroom?

Afghan Proverbs

- **Proverb:** Where your heart goes, there your feet will go.
  Meaning/Western Equivalent: Home is where the heart is.

- **Proverb:** No one says his/her own buttermilk is sour.
  Meaning/Western Equivalent: No one advertises his/her own faults.

- **Proverb:** Good perfume is known by its own scent rather than by the perfumer's advertisement.
  Meaning/Western Equivalent: The proof of the pudding is in the eating.

- **Proverb:** Without investigating the water, don't take off your shoes (to walk through it).
  Meaning/Western Equivalent: Look before you leap.

© Carson-Dellosa • CD-104263

Recipes

Ghraybeh Cookies (Swoon Cookies)

Ingredients:
½ cup (118 mL) cake flour
½ cup (118 mL) all-purpose flour
1 cup (237 mL) semolina flour
    (durum wheat flour may be substituted)
1 cup (237 mL) clarified butter
⅔ cup (158 mL) confectioners' sugar
¾ tsp. (4 mL) orange flower water
    (orange extract or orange zest may be
    substituted)
30 blanched almonds

Directions:
Preheat oven to 275ºF (140ºC). Sift the cake flour,
semolina, and all-purpose flour together and set
aside. Beat the butter for at least 10 minutes or until
fluffy. Then, beat for two more minutes while adding
the orange flower water and confectioners' sugar.
Gradually add the flour mixture. Refrigerate in a
covered bowl for approximately 10 minutes. On a
lightly floured surface, roll the dough to a thickness
of ¼" (0.6 cm) and cut into diamond shapes with sides
that are 1" (2.5 cm) each. Place ½" (1.25 cm) apart on an
ungreased baking sheet. Then, place an almond in the
center of each cookie. Bake for 35–40 minutes. Do not
overbake. Cool for at least one hour. Yield: 30 cookies

Fig and Date Bread

Ingredients:
1 cup (237 mL) chopped, pitted dates
1 cup (237 mL) chopped, dried figs
¼ cup (59 mL) unsalted butter, softened
1½ tsp. (8 mL) baking soda
1 cup (237 mL) water
½ cup (118 mL) granulated sugar
½ cup (118 mL) chopped walnuts
2 eggs
¾ cup (177 mL) all-purpose flour
¾ cup (177 mL) whole wheat flour
½ tsp. (3 mL) baking powder
½ tsp. (3 mL) salt

Directions:
Preheat oven to 350ºF (180ºC). Lightly grease an
8" x 4" (20.32 cm x 10.16 cm) loaf pan. In a medium bowl,
combine butter, figs, dates, and baking soda. Add water. Stir
well and let stand for 15 minutes. Add sugar, walnuts, and
eggs and stir. Combine the all-purpose flour, whole wheat
flour, baking powder, and salt in a separate bowl. Then, add
these ingredients to the date mixture and stir until blended.
Pour batter into the pan. Bake for 30–35 minutes. Remove
the pan from the oven and cover with aluminum foil. Lower
the oven temperature to 300ºF (150ºC). Return the bread
to the oven and bake for another 30–35 minutes or until a
toothpick inserted into the center comes out clean. Cool for
10 minutes, remove from pan, and place on a wire rack to
continue cooling. Yield: 8 servings

Classroom Activities

Go Fly a Kite!

Kite flying is known as *gudiparan bazi* in the Dari language. Many people in Afghanistan enjoy flying kites.

Materials:
8½" x 11" (21.59 cm x 27.94 cm) sheets of colorful or patterned paper
8" (20.32 cm) bamboo skewers or plastic drinking straws
1 roll plastic tape (such as florescent surveyor's flagging tape, available at hardware stores)
1 roll ½"-wide (1.27 cm) masking tape
1 roll string; 6'–10' (1.8 m–3 m) per child
1" x 3" (2.54 cm x 7.62 cm) pieces of cardboard on which to wrap the string
scissors
hole punch

Directions:
1. Have each student fold one sheet of colorful paper in half. (See Figure 1.)
2. Next, have her fold again along the diagonal line. (See Figure 2.)
3. Instruct each student to fold back one side, forming the kite shape (Figure 3) and place the masking tape firmly along the fold line between points A and B. (No stick or straw is needed here because the fold makes the paper stiff.)
4. Then, have each student place a bamboo stick or straw from point C to D and firmly tape it down with the masking tape. (See Figure 4.)
5. Instruct each student to cut 12"–18" (30.5 cm–46 cm) of plastic tape and attach it to the bottom of her kite at point B to make the kite's tail. (See Figure 5.)
6. Have each student turn her kite over on its back and fold the front flap back and forth until it stands straight.
7. Help each student punch a hole in the flap at point E, approximately ⅓ of the way down from point A. (See Figure 6.)
8. Finally, have each student tie one end of the string to the hole and wind the other end onto a piece of cardboard.

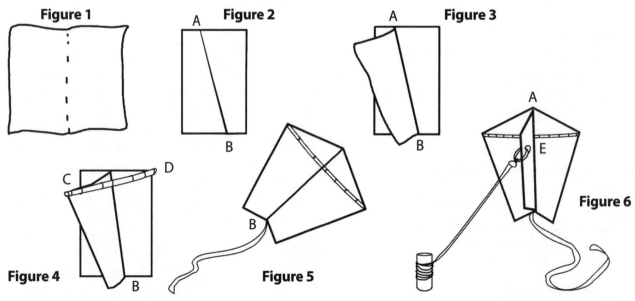

Figure 1

Figure 2

Figure 3

Figure 4

Figure 5

Figure 6

© Carson-Dellosa • CD-104263

Coloring Kites

Directions: Color each Afghan kite according to the color words in Pashto and English.

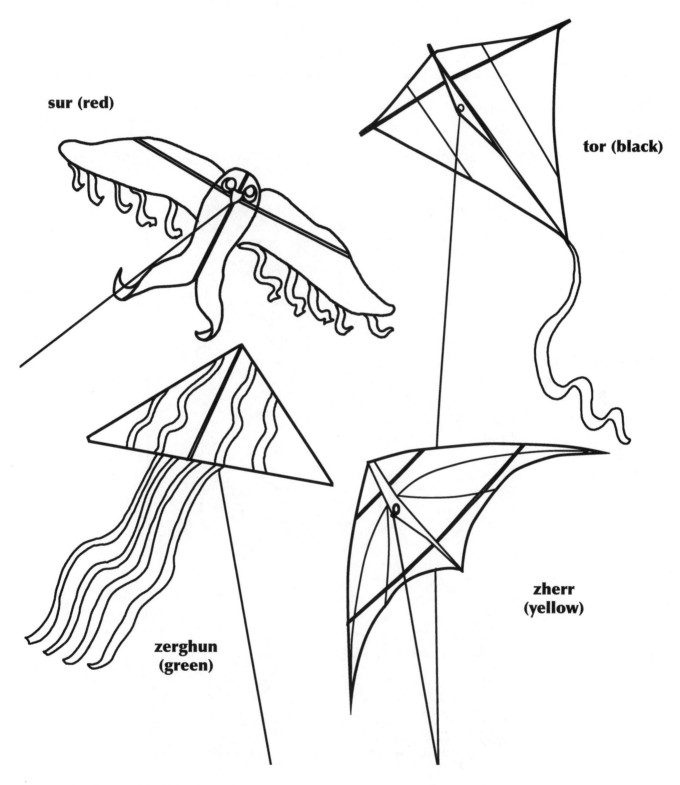

sur (red)

tor (black)

zherr (yellow)

zerghun (green)

Classroom Activities

Decorating an Afghan Rug

Many high-quality Afghan rugs are made in weaving centers in northern Afghan cities, such as Kunduz, Daulatabad, and Herat. Modern rugs from Afghanistan are descendants of rugs woven many generations ago in what is now the country of Turkmenistan. These rugs are usually red with black and ivory and sometimes have green or orange accents.

Name _____

Directions:

Color the Afghan rug below. Use colorful pencils, crayons, or markers. Display your colorful design in the classroom, in a hallway, or in the media center.

    © Carson-Dellosa • CD-104263

The Flag of Afghanistan

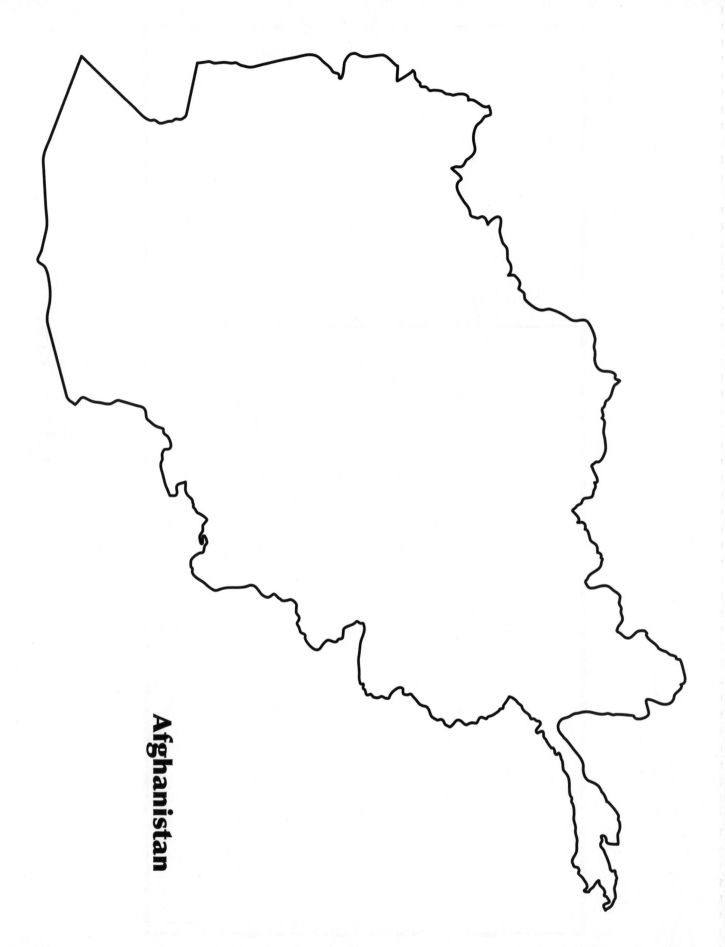

Afghanistan

© Carson-Dellosa • CD-104263

Additional Resources

Books

Abdullah, Morag Murray. *Valley of the Giant Buddhas*. Octagon Press, 1997.

Ali, Sharifah Enayat. *Cultures of the World: Afghanistan*. Benchmark Books, 2006.

Banting, Erinn. *Afghanistan: The Culture*. Crabtree Publishing, 2003.

Behnke, Alison. *Afghanistan in Pictures*. Lerner Publishing, 2003.

Dupree, Louis. *Afghanistan*. Oxford University Press, 2002.

Foster, Leila Merrell. *Afghanistan: Enchantment of the World*. Children's Press, 1996.

Harris, Y. L. *Hindu Kush*. Ashley Books, 1990.

Haskins, James and Kathleen Benson. *Count Your Way Through Afghanistan*. Millbrook Press, 2006.

Web Sites

CIA Word Factbook—Afghanistan.
https://www.cia.gov/library/publications/the-world-factbook/geos/af.html

Library of Congress Country Studies—Afghanistan.
http://lcweb2.loc.gov/frd/cs/aftoc.html

Lonely Planet—Afghanistan.
http://www.lonelyplanet.com/worldguide/destinations/asia/afghanistan

National Geographic—Afghanistan.
http://www3.nationalgeographic.com/places/countries/country_afghanistan.html

U.S. Department of State—Afghanistan.
http://www.state.gov/r/pa/ei/bgn/5380.htm

Approaching Ghana

Area: 89,166 sq. miles (230,940 sq. km)
Capital City: Accra
Population: 22,931,299
Main Languages: English, Asante, Ewe, and Fante
Main Religions: Christianity and Islam
Currency: Cedi
Government: Constitutional democracy
Flag:

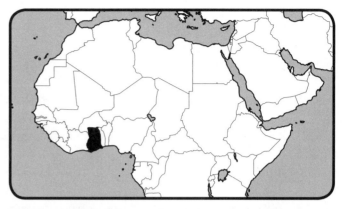

The flag of Ghana was adopted in 1957. It has three horizontal stripes of red, yellow, and green with a black star in the center stripe. The red stripe symbolizes the country's struggle for independence, the yellow stripe symbolizes the wealth of the country, and the green stripe symbolizes its forests and farms.

For Your Information

Ghana is located in West Africa, 400 miles (644 kilometers) north of the equator. It is approximately the same size as the United Kingdom. Three countries form Ghana's land borders: the Ivory Coast to the west; Togo to the east; and Burkina Faso to the north and northwest. The southern border is formed by the Gulf of Guinea. Ghana has five main geographical regions. The southern coastline contains low plains. North of these plains are the Ashanti Uplands, the Volta Basin, and the Akwapim-Togo Ranges. The high plains are in the northern and northwestern part of the country.

The climate of Ghana is always warm, with average temperatures above 80°F (27°C). There are two seasons: rainy and dry. Some parts of Ghana receive as much as 83 inches (211 centimeters) of rain per year, while other parts of Ghana receive less than 40 inches (101 centimeters). Ghana is affected by two large air masses: one that flows south from the Sahara and another that flows north from the Atlantic Ocean.

The largest man-made lake and reservoir in the world is Lake Volta in Ghana. Lake Volta is Ghana's most noticeable geographic feature. It is 250 miles (402 kilometers) long and has an average width of 16 miles (26 kilometers). The lake was created in 1966 when the Akosombo Dam was built on the Volta River. The lake provides transportation, hydroelectric power, and water for irrigation.

A wide variety of wildlife can be found in Ghana, including leopards, lions, elephants, antelope, monkeys, hippopotamuses, and crocodiles. Many types of birds and fish are also found in Ghana. Several areas of the country have been set aside as wildlife parks and national parks. The Owabi Wildlife Sanctuary, Mole National Park, Gbelle Game Reserve, the Kujani Game Reserve, and the Kakum National Park are some of these parks.

One of the best known foods is called *fufu*, which is a starchy food made of yams. Yams are an important part of the diet in Ghana. Fufu is difficult to prepare. The yams are boiled, peeled, and then pounded into a sticky mixture. Often, two women work together to prepare this dish because the yams are difficult to pound as they are cooked.

© Carson-Dellosa • CD-104263

Fascinating Facts

A brilliant, colorful fabric known as *Kente* is the most well-known cloth produced in Ghana. Ghanaian weavers use bright colors and intricate designs to make handwoven Kente cloth. These cloths are usually worn for ceremonies, festivals, and other special occasions. Women wear the cloth in two pieces. One piece is wound around the waist to form a floor-length skirt and is worn with a blouse. The other piece is used as a shawl or hung loosely over the arm.

The Baobab tree is an unusual tree that the people of Ghana use in a variety of ways. This tree grows throughout Africa in the savanna (grassland) region. The Baobab tree looks as if it has been turned upside down, with its roots sticking up in the air and the branches buried in the soil. The tree can grow to a height of 60 feet (18 meters) and have a diameter of 30 feet (9 meters). The fruit, which can be eaten, is large and gourd-like. The trunk is often cut and hollowed out to make barrels for the collection and storage of rainwater. The bark is used to make cloth and rope. The tree also provides shade.

Kofi Annan, a Ghanaian, became known worldwide when he was named as the secretary-general of the United Nations in 1997. His term began with a crisis in Iraq. Before serving in the United Nations, Annan joined the World Health Organization in 1962 and served as a clerk in Geneva, Switzerland. Annan became the secretary-general at a time of crisis for the United Nations. The United Nations was in serious debt because more than half of the member states were not paying their contributions.

The largest city in Ghana is the capital, Accra. This city has a population of more than 1.5 million people. Except for a few hills like the one on which the University of Ghana is located, the landscape of Ghana is mostly flat. Accra's economy is based on its busy port and the manufacture of clothing, timber, plywood, and processed food. The Makola Market, located in the center of Accra, is the city's main shopping district. This market is a collection of stalls where people can buy almost anything they need, from clothing to food to household goods.

Ghana is one of the most important producers of cocoa beans in the world. Cocoa is grown in the middle of the country, south of the Black Volta River. *Cacao* (cocoa) is the basic ingredient for chocolate. Before it is processed and turned into chocolate bars or other candies, the cocoa bean is quite bitter. When conditions are right, Ghana produces as much as 385,800 tons (350,000 metric tons) of cocoa beans in a single growing season. Thousands of Ghanaians work on cocoa farms.

Known as the "Gold Coast" when it was a colony of Great Britain, Ghana has been associated with gold for more than 500 years. Gold mined in Ghana was sold and shipped to Europe across the Sahara. The Obuasi gold mine in the Asante region has been in operation since 1907. Even though it might seem like every gold mine would make a profit, some gold mines are more profitable than others. The older and deeper the mine, the more it costs to remove the gold.

© Carson-Dellosa • CD-104263

Language Activities

The Asante language commonly spoken in Ghana is actually one of two dialects of the Akan language.

Asante Words and Phrases

abusua	mother's family	*kente*	handwoven Asante cloth
abusuapanyin	family leader or family head	*kontomire*	form of spinach
ahenemma	royal sandals	*kpanlogo*	traditional conga-shaped drum
akondwa	seat	*nkita*	a stew of eggs, fish, and beef
akuaba	wooden dolls	*nkuro*	town
Asantehene	title of the king of the Asante	*oman*	state
Asanteman	the state of Asante	*sika futuro*	gold dust
kelewele	fried plantains	*tartare*	plantain pancakes

Ghanaian Proverbs

- **Proverb:** Although the rain soaks the leopard's spots, it does not wash them off.
  Meaning: No matter what happens, a person's true nature does not change.

- **Proverb:** Never rub up against a porcupine.
  Meaning: Do not start a fight with someone more powerful than you, because you will probably lose.

- **Proverb:** People who follow an elephant do not get wet from the dew.
  Meaning: Powerful men and women protect their followers.

- **Proverb:** While other trees lose their leaves, the palm tree's leaves will always remain fresh.
  Meaning: A wish for long life and prosperity

- **Proverb:** When a shield wears out, its framework remains.
  Meaning: Although all people pass away, their good deeds and wisdom live on.

- **Proverb:** The knot that is tied by a wise man cannot be untied by a fool.
  Meaning: The leader has a right to his position because of his special wisdom.

- **Proverb:** Power is like an egg: when held firmly, it does not break. But when held loosely, it falls from your grasp and breaks into pieces.
  Meaning: It is necessary to keep a tight grip on power.

© Carson-Dellosa • CD-104263

Recipes

Kelewele (Fried Plantains)

Ingredients:
3 large, ripe plantains
½ cup (118 mL) vegetable oil
½ cup (118 mL) super fine sugar
2 tsp. (10 mL) freshly grated nutmeg
1 tbsp. (15 mL) ground cinnamon
1 tbsp. (15 mL) finely grated orange zest
salt
sour cream

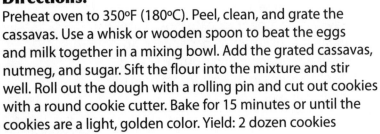

Directions:
1. Preheat oven to 300ºF (150ºC).
2. Cut vertically through the skin of each plantain, but do not cut the inside. Peel off the skin and remove the ends.
3. Place each plantain on a cutting board and slice diagonally into ¾" (1.9 cm) thick slices.
4. Place these slices into cold water with ½ tsp. (2.5 mL) salt and set aside.
5. Heat the vegetable oil in a nonstick pan on medium to medium-high heat.
6. Drain the plantain slices and pat dry with paper towels. Then, place slices into hot oil and fry.
7. Remove the plantain slices when they are golden brown on both sides.
8. Place the slices on paper towels to drain.
9. Place the slices in an ovenproof dish and cover with aluminum foil. Then, place in a preheated oven to keep warm.
10. In a separate bowl, mix the sugar, cinnamon, and nutmeg.
11. Arrange the plantain slices on a serving plate and sprinkle with the sugar mixture and orange zest.
12. Serve with warm sour cream. Yield: 4–6 servings

Gari Biscuits

Ingredients:
5 medium cassavas or yucas
3 eggs
½ cup (118 mL) whole milk
¾ cup (177 mL) sugar
1 tsp. (5 mL) nutmeg
1 tbsp. (15 mL) flour

Directions:
Preheat oven to 350ºF (180ºC). Peel, clean, and grate the cassavas. Use a whisk or wooden spoon to beat the eggs and milk together in a mixing bowl. Add the grated cassavas, nutmeg, and sugar. Sift the flour into the mixture and stir well. Roll out the dough with a rolling pin and cut out cookies with a round cookie cutter. Bake for 15 minutes or until the cookies are a light, golden color. Yield: 2 dozen cookies

Classroom Activities

Kpanlogo Drum

The *kpanlogo*, a traditional conga-shaped drum, is used in Ghana to accompany the Kpanlogo dance of the Ewe tribe. This drum is made with a variety of animal skins. Each skin gives the drum a unique sound. Often, the drum is made using cow skin. Sometimes, antelope or goat skin is used. The drum can be raised off the floor with a person's legs as it is played. Raising the drum changes the tone. Players can achieve a variety of tones depending on where the top of the drum is struck. Deep base tones can be made by striking the top of the drum near the edge while higher tones can be made by striking it in the center.

Making an African Drum

Materials:
large coffee cans (or other empty cans or cylindrical containers)
construction paper
scraps of cloth
glue
glitter
beads
tempera paint
paintbrushes
drumsticks or dowel rods

Directions:
1. Have each student cut a rectangle of construction paper or cloth to cover the outside of his empty can.
2. Instruct each student to draw patterns of lines, dots, or animal shapes on the construction paper or cloth scrap. Encourage him to repeat patterns where possible to create a more attractive design.
3. Tell each student to cover and glue the paper or cloth to the outside of his empty can.
4. Using paint, glitter, beads, or other craft materials, have each student decorate the outside of his drum.
5. Have each student repeat steps 1–3 with a square of construction paper or scrap cloth to cover the opening of his drum.
6. Display drums in the classroom or in the media center.

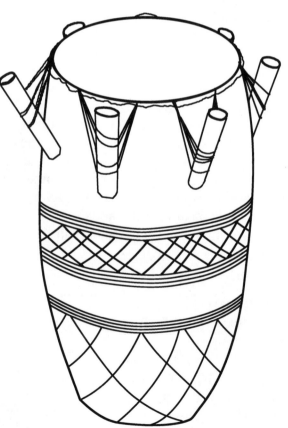

© Carson-Dellosa • CD-104263

Classroom Activities

Making a Kente Design

Ghanaians have woven Kente cloth for more than 400 years. The word *kente* comes from the word *kenten*, which means "basket." The first Kente weavers used raffia fibers and wove them into a cloth that looked like a basket. Each design has a proverbial meaning. Men wear the cloth in much the same way as the ancient Greeks wore togas, while women wear the cloth as two separate pieces.

Kente cloths are woven by hand in the colors that represent Africa:

> red = life and blood
> gold = strength and fortune
> green = Mother Africa or Mother Earth
> blue = innocence
> black = people and unity

Materials:
library books or Web sites about African
      and Ghanaian Kente cloth designs
large brown paper grocery bags
scissors
colorful pencils, crayons, and markers
rulers
pencils

Directions:
1. As a class, use reference books or Web sites to research traditional Ghanaian Kente cloth designs.
2. Have each student cut off the bottom of her grocery bag.
3. Then, have each student cut her bag down the center.
4. Instruct each student to cut a hole in each side to form arm openings.
5. Next, have each student use a ruler and a pencil to draw a design similar to one of the Kente designs she researched.
6. Have each student color her design using red, blue, green, black, and/or gold.
7. Let each student model the Kente vest she has created for the class.
8. Display students' completed vests on a bulletin board.

© Carson-Dellosa • CD-104263

Map Activity

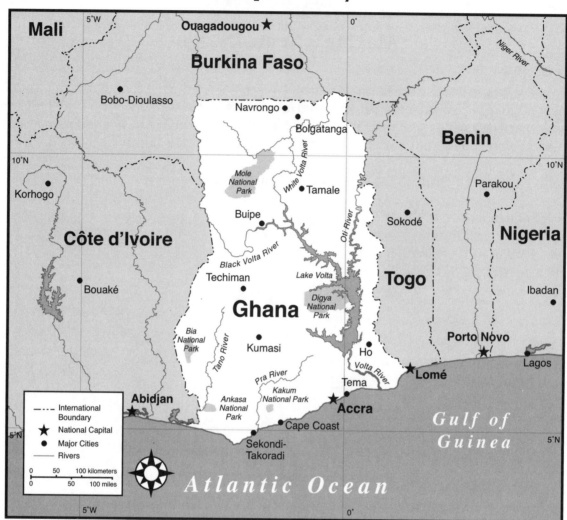

Directions: Use the map to answer the questions.

1. This city is located on the Black Volta River.
   A. Tema   B. Buipe   C. Tamale   D. Navrongo

2. The city of Buipe is located north of the city of _____.
   A. Navrongo   B. Tamale   C. Bolgatanga   D. Techiman

3. Cape Coast is located about _____ miles southwest of the capital city of Accra.
   A. 100   B. 50   C. 75   D. 30

4. The _____ National Park is located east of the city of Techiman.
   A. Bia   B. Digya   C. Mole   D. Ankasa

5. The country of _____ borders Ghana to the east.
   A. Togo   B. Côte d'Ivoire   C. Burkina Faso   D. Mali

© Carson-Dellosa • CD-104263

Name _____

Word Search

Directions: Find the words from the Word Bank in the word search. Words can go across, down, or diagonally.

Word Bank

Accra	Christianity	gold	kpanlogo
Akan	cocoa	Islam	Lake Volta
Akosombo Dam	fufu	Kente	plantain

```
O  C  K  F  K  Q  A  G  O  L  D  Y  H  F  C
B  O  A  E  U  L  F  T  E  F  T  E  J  E  E
X  C  X  P  N  F  C  B  B  I  M  R  P  L  C
Y  O  R  L  V  T  U  Y  N  O  A  C  C  R  A
M  A  C  A  M  D  E  A  N  F  V  Z  Q  L  Q
G  I  V  N  B  I  I  C  Y  C  Q  E  K  R  G
O  W  U  T  L  T  I  Q  L  S  B  M  R  U  X
B  J  M  A  S  D  O  T  M  O  A  O  K  A  O
W  S  A  I  N  O  L  P  D  L  I  E  B  G  S
J  C  R  N  Y  A  F  U  S  X  I  E  O  W  D
S  H  N  E  T  Y  X  I  W  D  T  L  A  V  I
C  G  L  E  V  K  E  F  L  F  N  E  K  K  P
A  K  O  S  O  M  B  O  D  A  M  E  A  H  W
Q  A  R  N  L  Z  K  K  P  B  P  B  N  S  G
P  W  Z  R  J  L  A  K  E  V  O  L  T  A  Q
```

© Carson-Dellosa • CD-104263

The Flag of Ghana

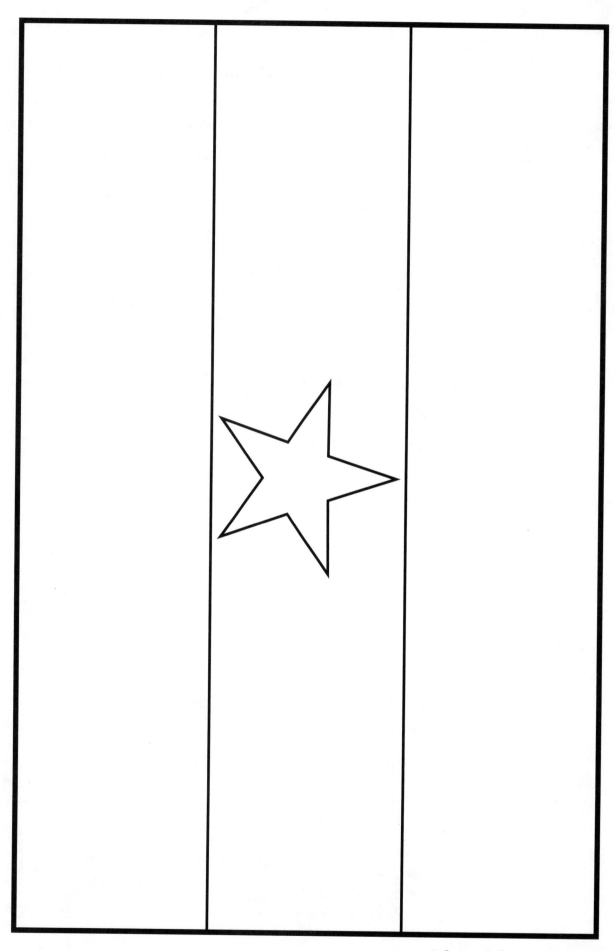

© Carson-Dellosa • CD-104263

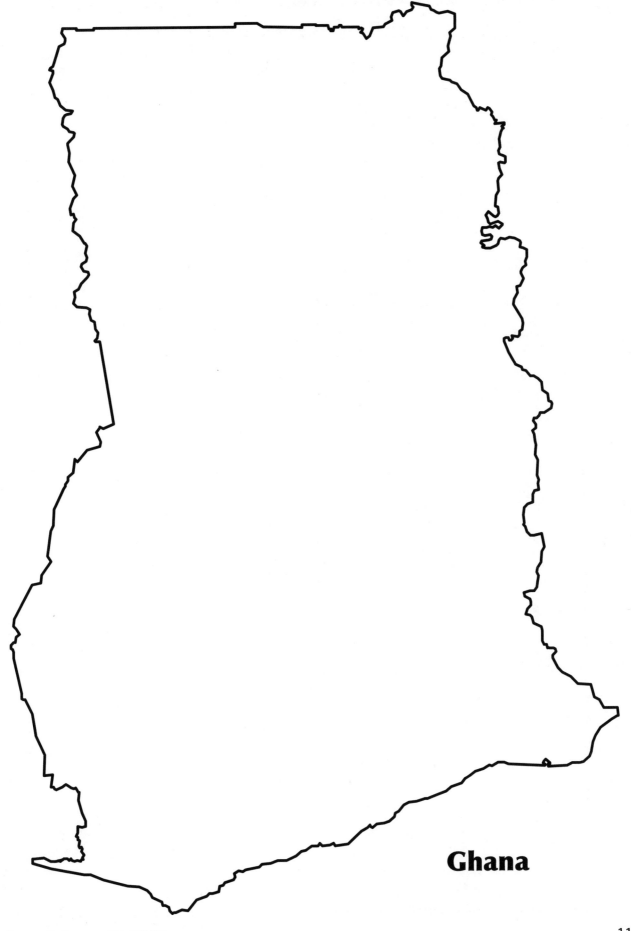

Ghana

© Carson-Dellosa • CD-104263

Additional Resources

Books

Ahiagble, Gilbert and Louise Meyer. *Master Weaver from Ghana*. Open Hand Publishing, 1998.

Blauer, Ettagale and Jason Lauré. *Ghana: Enchantment of the World*. Children's Press, 1999.

Boateng, Faustina Ama. *Asante*. The Rosen Publishing Group, Inc., 1996.

Gocking, Roger S. *The History of Ghana*. Greenwood Press, 2005.

Kuada, John and Yao Chachah. *Ghana: Understanding the People and Their Culture*. Woeli Publishing, 1999.

Lapierre, Yvette. *Ghana in Pictures*. Lerner Publishing, 2004.

Levy, Patricia. *Cultures of the World: Ghana*. Benchmark Books, 1999.

Web Sites

Africa Guide—Ghana.
http://www.africaguide.com/country/ghana/

BBC News—Ghana.
http://news.bbc.co.uk/1/hi/world/africa/country_profiles/1023355.stm

CIA World Factbook—Ghana.
https://www.cia.gov/library/publications/the-world-factbook/geos/gh.html

Geographia.com—Ghana.
http://www.geographia.com/ghana/

Library of Congress Country Studies—Ghana.
http://lcweb2.loc.gov/frd/cs/ghtoc.html

Lonely Planet—Ghana.
http://www.lonelyplanet.com/worldguide/destinations/africa/ghana/

 © Carson-Dellosa • CD-104263

Last Stop: Morocco

Area: 172,317 sq. miles (446,300 sq. km)
Capital City: Rabat
Population: 33,757,175
Main Languages: Arabic, Berber, French
Main Religion: Islam
Currency: Moroccan dirham
Government: Constitutional monarchy
Flag:

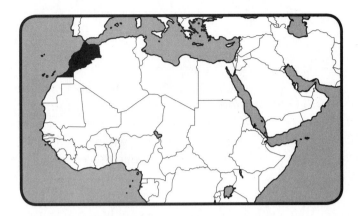

The design of Morocco's flag was first created in 1912. It has a red background with a green outlined star in the center known as the "Seal of Solomon." The green represents Islam (the official religion of Morocco) because it is the color of nature. Red represents the reigning Moroccan dynasty.

For Your Information

Morocco is located in the northwestern corner of Africa. It is slightly larger than the state of California. The western boundary is formed by the Atlantic Ocean, and the northern boundary is formed by the Mediterranean Sea. To the east and southeast is the country of Algeria. Western Sahara extends along the southern end of the country.

There are four geographic regions in Morocco. In the north, the Rif Mountains parallel the Mediterranean coast and rise to a height of 8,000 feet (2,438 meters). The Atlas Mountains extend across the country from the southwest to the northeast between the Atlantic Ocean and the Rif Mountains. A wide coastal plain extends along the country's western seaboard. This is where most Moroccans live. South of the Atlas Mountains are the lowlands, which merge with the Sahara.

Because of Morocco's varied geology and rich mineral deposits, it is one of the world's largest exporters of phosphates. These phosphates are used to produce traditional ceramic tiles and pottery. There are four main centers for the production of pottery in Morocco. In the far north, the rich red soil of Wadi Lan is the raw material used to create unglazed terra-cotta pottery. Yellowish clay that is used to create pottery is found on the banks of the Bou Regreg River in the Rabat region. Fez is famous for the production of blue pottery known by the local people as *Fakhari*.

Morocco's climate is dry, although small amounts of rain do fall between November and March. The temperatures vary greatly depending on the season and location within the country. In the southern and southeastern desert regions, temperatures can be extremely high during the hot summer months. In the higher altitudes of the mountains, it is cool on summer evenings and freezing on winter evenings.

About one-half of Morocco's workforce is employed in agriculture. In the rainy sections of the northeast, wheat and other grains are raised without the use of irrigation. On the Atlantic coast, olives, citrus fruits, and grapes are grown in the plains with water supplied by artesian wells. Oranges are the most important crop, but Morocco is also well-known for its tangerines and lemons.

Fascinating Facts

The origin of the *tarboosh* or *fez* hat is not clear. The design may have originated in ancient Greece or in the Balkans. The fez gained wide acceptance when the Ottoman rulers modernized traditional costumes. Because the brimless hat did not get in the way of the daily prayers of the Muslims, and it was cleaner and less awkward than the turban, the fez became popular. The name *fez* is believed to have come from the city of Fez, which once produced the red dye used in making the hat.

In Morocco, a hostess might take a week to prepare a meal for her honored guests. The meal may have as many as 50 courses. The dinner begins with *Bstilla*, a crisp pastry filled with chicken. Preparations for the Bstilla take an entire day. The next course would be *tajine*, which is chicken or meat in a spicy stew served with a flat bread called *Khubz*.

The largest port in Morocco is the city of Casablanca. It is also an important industrial center. Some of the major industries include textile and leather good manufacturing, oil refining, and food processing. The city was founded in the 12th century. In the 1700s, a huge earthquake destroyed much of the city, and it had to be rebuilt. In Casablanca, the average temperature in January is 55°F (13°C). In July, the average temperature is 72°F (22°C).

Goulimine beads are made of glass and beautifully decorated. The beads were named for the southern city of Goulimine, which was a vital link in the caravan route to Timbuktu. The beads look like a bouquet of flowers in glass. At one time, the beads were highly treasured by African chiefs. Huge baskets of Goulimine beads could be found for sale in every city. Now, the best beads are very rare and expensive.

Moroccan carpets are made in rural areas and cities. In the mountains and desert areas, Berber carpets are woven by women. However, in the cities, they are woven by Arab men. These carpets are known for their intricate patterns and colors. The carpets can be identified by the region in which they were made because each tribal group uses a different pattern.

Moroccan mint tea is a part of every meal. The tea is usually served from a silver teapot and poured into small glasses. Part of the pleasure of drinking the tea is enjoying the art of pouring it. The tea is always poured from a great distance above the glass—usually as much as two feet (61 centimeters). The use of fresh mint balances the sugar and makes a delicious combination.

The port of Tangier is often called the "gateway to Africa." The city is at least 3,000 years old. More than 2,000 years ago, the city was an important trading center. Strategically located on the Strait of Gibraltar, Tangier was a rich target for anyone wanting to control access to the Mediterranean Sea and the Atlantic Ocean. Tangier is one of the most visited cities in Morocco. More than 1 million people visit this site each year. Some Moroccans want to build a bridge from Tangier across the Strait of Gibraltar to Spain. This bridge would be 25 miles (40 kilometers) long.

© Carson-Dellosa • CD-104263

Arabic Language Activities

Alphabet

alif	ا	dal	د	daad	ض	khaf	ك
ba	ب	zal	ذ	tah	ط	lam	ل
ta	ت	ra	ر	zah	ظ	mim	م
tha	ث	zay	ز	eyn	ع	noon	ن
jem	ج	sín	س	ghyn	غ	ha	ه
ha	ح	shin	ش	pha	ف	waw	و
kha	خ	saad	ص	qaf	ق	ya	ي

Numbers

١	٢	٣	٤	٥
1	2	3	4	5

٦	٧	٨	٩	١٠
6	7	8	9	10

Days of the Week

Al-Ithnan	Monday
Al-Toulata	Tuesday
Al-Arbya	Wednesday
Al-Khamees	Thursday
Al-Jumah	Friday
Al-Sabt	Saturday
Al-Ahad	Sunday

Everyday Expressions and Words

salam-aly-kum	hello	jyed	fine	ma-salama	good-bye
nam	yes	oum	mother	ustaz	teacher
la	no	ab	father	madrasaa	school
min fadlik	please	akh	brother	bait	home
shukran	thank you	ukht	sister	ta'ra	airplane
Kaf-ha-lik	How are you?	sadeek	friend	felous	money

© Carson-Dellosa • CD-104263

Recipes

Batinjaan Zalud (Eggplant Salad)

Ingredients:
1 or 2 large eggplants, approx. 2 lbs. (0.91 kg) total
3 cloves garlic, finely chopped
4 tbsp. (59 mL) lemon juice
1 tsp. (5 mL) salt
¼ tsp. (1 mL) ground pepper
1 tbsp. (15 mL) sugar
½ cup (118 mL) vegetable oil
¼ cup (59 mL) onion, finely chopped
½ tsp. (2.5 mL) olive oil
1 tomato, sliced
8 black olives

Directions:
Peel the eggplants. Cut into 1" (2.54 cm) slices. In a 10" (25.4 cm) pan, fry the slices in the vegetable oil until soft. Mash the eggplant. Add the onion, garlic, lemon juice, salt, pepper, and sugar and mix well. Chill in the refrigerator for at least one hour. Heap ½ cup (118 mL) eggplant mixture on a plate. Mash to form a "pancake." Drizzle with olive oil if mixture appears dry. Then, place one tomato slice in the center of the circle and one black olive in the center of the tomato. Yield: 8 small salads

Mint Tea

Ingredients:
2–3 tsp. (10–15 mL) green tea
20 sugar cubes
fresh mint sprigs
2 qt. (1.893 L) water

Directions:
Pour ¼ cup (59 mL) boiling water into a large teapot. Swish the water around to warm the pot. Add the green tea and desired amount of sugar and fill the teapot with the rest of the boiling water. Let steep for five minutes. Add mint. Pour tea through a tea strainer and serve in glasses. Yield: 8–12 servings

© Carson-Dellosa • CD-104263

Classroom Activities

Making a Fez Hat

Materials:
paper bags
glue or glue sticks
scissors
25" (63.5 cm) pieces of black yarn (12 pieces per student)
red markers/crayons

Directions:

1. Show students an enlarged copy of the fez hat drawing (above). Then, have each student open a bag and place it beside her head to see if it is the right size. If the bag is too long, have her roll the bag upward or trim the bag to the desired size.
2. Instruct each student to color her bag red.
3. Help each student use 12 yarn pieces to create a tassel for her hat. Align all of the yarn pieces so that the ends are even. Use one piece to tie the other pieces together at the center, leaving a long tail. Hold the whole bundle by this tail, so that the rest of the pieces of yarn hang down. Cut 2" (5.08 cm) of yarn from the tail. Tie the 2" (5.08 cm) yarn piece around the top of the yarn bundle.
4. Have each student attach the tassel to her "hat" by first poking a hole in the top center of the bag. Then, have her thread the tail of the tassel through the hole and tie off the tail so that the tassel will stay in place.
5. Have a fez parade so that students can show off their Moroccan hats.

Classroom Activities

Making a Good Luck Hand

In Morocco, one symbol of good luck is known as the *Khamsa*. This symbol has been used as an amulet in North Africa for hundreds of years. Often, it is made from a precious metal, such as silver. In Arabic, *Khamsa* means "five." For this reason, the Khamsa is a picture of a hand showing five fingers.

Materials:
construction paper (2 sheets per student)
scissors
pencils
crayons, markers, or colorful pencils
glitter
sequins

Directions:
1. Have each student use a pencil to trace his hand on a sheet of construction paper.
2. Next, have each student cut out the tracing of his hand.
3. Instruct each student to glue his hand tracing to the center of another piece of construction paper.
4. Have each student draw designs on the hand, such as geometric shapes, animals, or other things from nature.
5. Then, have each student use crayons, markers, or colorful pencils to color his lucky hand.
6. Next, have each student decorate his hand with glitter, sequins, etc.
7. Display the Khamsas in the classroom, in a hallway, or in the media center.
8. Direct each student to write a story about his good luck hand.

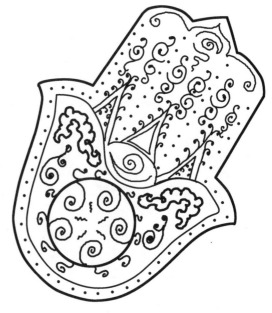

© Carson-Dellosa • CD-104263

Counting Moroccan Rugs

Directions: Draw a line to match each group of Moroccan rugs with the correct Arabic number. Color the rugs. On the back of your paper, write descriptions of the colors and patterns found in some of your rugs.

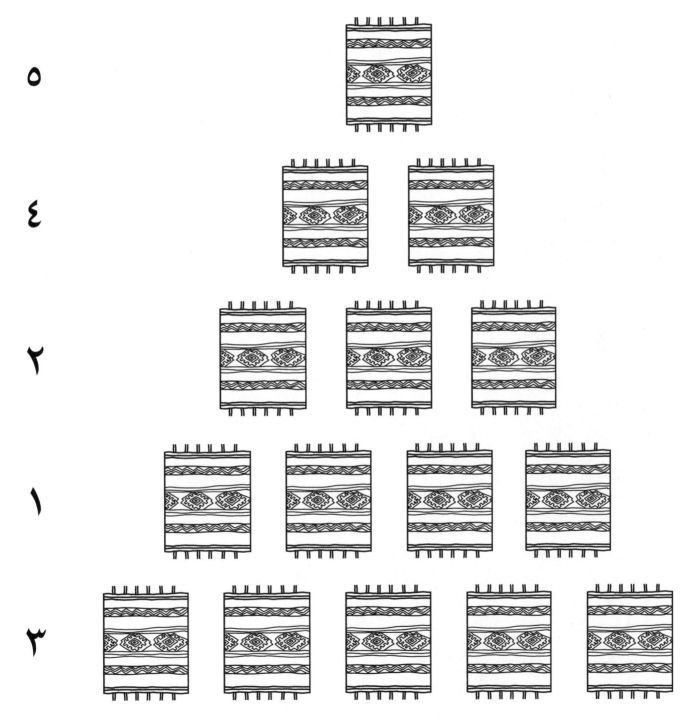

Crossword Puzzle

Directions: Complete the crossword puzzle using the clues.

Across:
2. Morocco's main religion
6. a major desert in Morocco
7. a type of tea Moroccans drink with every meal
8. mountains that extend across Morocco
9. a type of hat named after a Moroccan city
10. the main language spoken in Morocco
11. the capital city of Morocco

Down:
1. the currency used in Morocco
3. a good luck symbol in North Africa
4. the country's largest port and industrial center
5. a craft made in four regions of Morocco

© Carson-Dellosa • CD-104263

The Flag of Morocco

© Carson-Dellosa • CD-104263

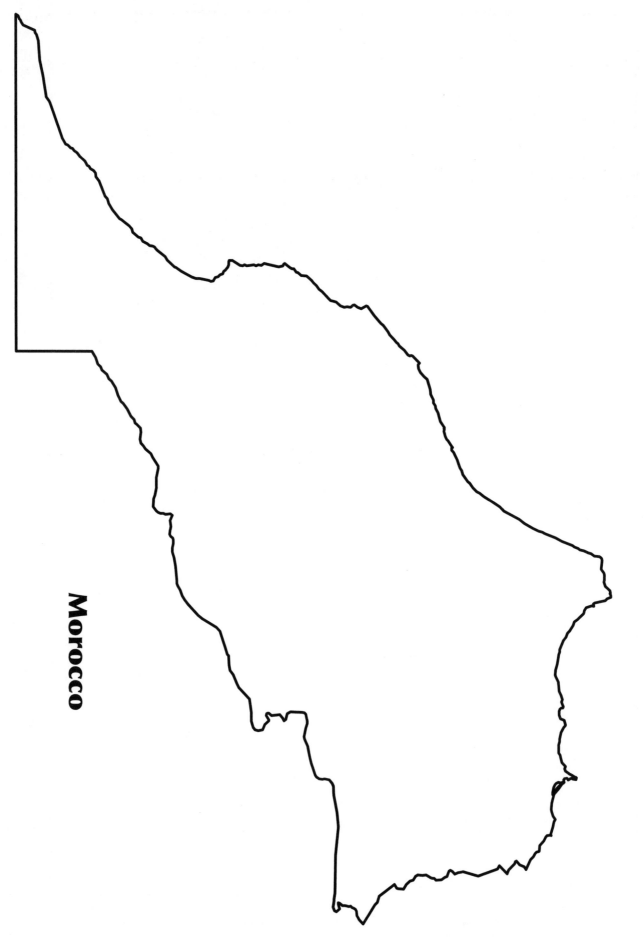

Morocco

124

© Carson-Dellosa • CD-104263

Additional Resources

Books

Blauer, Ettagale and Jason Laure. *Morocco: Enchantment of the World*. Children's Press, 1999.

Delgado, Kevin. *Morocco: Modern Nations of the World*. Lucent Books, 2006.

DiPiazza, Francesca Davis. *Morocco in Pictures*. Twenty-First Century Books, 2002.

Fordyce, Deborah. *Welcome to Morocco*. Gareth Stevens Publishing, 2004.

Geography Department. *Morocco in Pictures*. Lerner Publishing, 1993.

Johnson-Davies, Denys. *Tales From Morocco*. Amideast, 1995.

Seward, Pat. *Morocco: Modern Nations of the World*. Benchmark Books, 2006.

Wilkins, Frances. *Morocco: Major World Nations*. Chelsea House, 1999.

Web Sites

BBC News—Morocco.
http://news.bbc.co.uk/1/hi/world/middle_east/country_profiles/791867.stm

CIA World Factbook—Morocco.
https://www.cia.gov/library/publications/the-world-factbook/geos/mo.html

Geographia.com—Morocco.
http://www.geographia.com/morocco/

Lonely Planet—Morocco.
http://www.lonelyplanet.com/worldguide/destinations/africa/morocco/

U. S. Department of State—Morocco.
http://www.state.gov/r/pa/ei/bgn/5431.htm

Embassies in the United States

Teach students that embassies are organizations that conduct foreign relations with host governments. A host government is the government of the country where an embassy is located. Embassies also give visas to people allowing them to travel to their home countries. Ambassadors, who are in charge of embassies, are representatives of their countries.

Embassy of Afghanistan
2341 Wyoming Avenue, NW
Washington, DC 20008
Phone: 202-483-6410
Fax: 202-483-6488
E-mail: *info@embassyofafghanistan.org*

Embassy of Chile
1732 Massachusetts Avenue, NW
Washington, DC 20036
Phone: 202-785-1746
Fax: 202-887-5579
E-mail: *embassy@embassyofchile.org*

Embassy of Cuba
2630 16th Street, NW
Washington, DC 20009
Phone: 202-797-8518
Fax: 202-986-7283
E-mail: *cubaseccion@igc.apc.org*

Embassy of Ghana
3512 International Drive, NW
Washington, DC 20008
Phone: 202-686-4520
Fax: 202-686-4527
E-mail: *info@ghanaembassy.org*

Embassy of Guatemala
2220 R Street, NW
Washington, DC 20008
Phone: 202-745-4952
Fax: 202-745-1908
E-mail: *info@guatemala-embassy.org*

Embassy of Iraq
1801 P Street, NW
Washington, DC 20036
Phone: 202-483-7500
Fax: 202-462-5066
E-mail: *usconsulbaghdad@state.gov*

Embassy of Morocco
1601 21st Street, NW
Washington, DC 20009
Phone: 202-462-7979
Fax: 202-265-0161
E-mail: *info@moroccanconsulate.com*

Embassy of Norway
2720 34th Street, NW
Washington, DC 20008
Phone: 202-333-6000
Fax: 202-337-0870
E-mail: *emb.washington@mfa.no*

Embassy of Peru
1700 Massachusetts Avenue, NW
Washington, DC 20036
Phone: 202-833-9860
Fax: 202-659-8124
E-mail: *webmaster@embassyofperu.us*

Embassy of Spain
2375 Pennsylvania Avenue, NW
Washington, DC 20037
Phone: 202-452-0100
Fax: 202-833-5670
E-mail: *spain@spainemb.org*

Embassy of the United Kingdom
3100 Massachusetts Avenue, NW
Washington, DC 20008
Phone: 202-588-6500
Fax: 202-588-7870
Web Site: *www.britainusa.com*

© Carson-Dellosa • CD-104263

Answer Key

Page 12

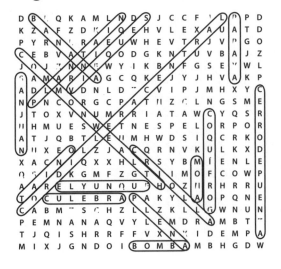

Page 21

Each bird should be colored according to the directions.

Page 22

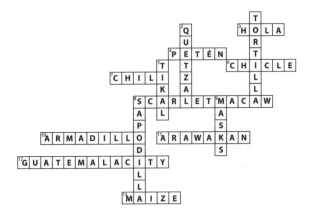

Page 32

1. B, 2. C, 3. D, 4. D, 5. A, 6. D

Page 33

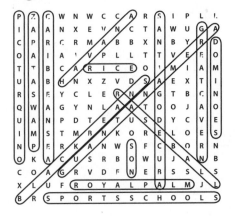

Page 42

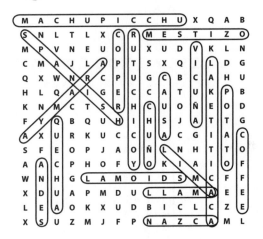

Page 50

1. Easter Island, 2. Santiago, 3. Robinson,
4. Fiestas Patrias, 5. Day of the Dead, 6. chub,
7. peso, 8. Huasos, Puzzle Answer: Pablo Neruda

Answer Key

Page 62

```
C A S T I L I A N
L
H
A
M       I B E R I A N
B       B
R       R       M U L H A C É N
P A M P L O N A       A
E       R       D
S       T O R E R O S
E U R O       I
T       C       D
A L C Á Z A R
          N
          L A T O M A T I N A
          R
          P Y R E N E E S
```

Page 72

1. C, 2. B, 3. C, 4. C, 5. A, 6. D

Page 80

1. C, 2. B, 3. A, 4. C, 5. D, 6. C, 7. D, 8. C, 9. A, 10. D

Page 90

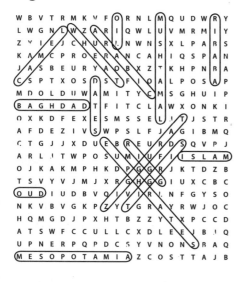

Page 99

Each kite should be colored according its label.

Page 110

1. B, 2. D, 3. C, 4. B, 5. A

Page 111

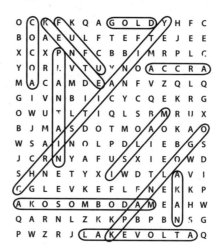

Page 121

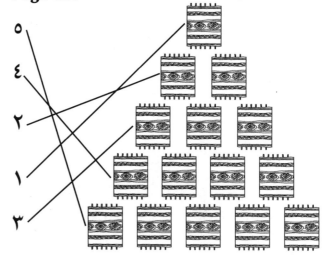

Page 122

```
D
I S L A M
R       K
H   C   H       P
S A H A R A   O
M   S   M I N T   T
    A T L A S   F E Z
    B   A   T
    A R A B I C R
    N       Y
    C
    R A B A T
```

© Carson-Dellosa • CD-104263